Bonsai, Saikei and Bonkei

Bonsai, Saikei and Bonkei

Japanese Dwarf Trees and Tray Landscapes

by Robert Lee Behme

All photographs by the author except the two noted

William Morrow & Company, Inc.
425 Park Avenue South · New York, N.Y. 10016

Published simultaneously in Canada by George J. McLeod Limited, Toronto.

Printed in the United States of America.

Library of Congress Catalog Card Number 68-56412

Acknowledgments

This book could never have been completed without the generous assistance of Yoshio Sato and Peter Ioka. Mr. Sato, owner of the University Nursery in Berkeley, California, gave me the courage to begin and then a full measure of critical judgment. Mr. Ioka of the American Bonsai Society shared his interest in bonsai and expanded my knowledge of bonkei. Many photographs of Mr. Sato's and Mr. Ioka's bonsai appear in this book.

I wish also to express my gratitude: *to Frank Williams for the beautiful designing of this book.*

To John A. Dutro of the East Bay Bonsai Club, who drew freely for me from a well of practical experience and also permitted me to photograph many of his bonsai; To Arnoldine Small who shared her knowledge of native material with its possibilities for unusual bonsai; To Henry Matsutani, who checked part of my manuscript for accuracy, and also supplied bonsai for photographing; To Connie and Horace Hinds of the Kusamura Bonsai Club and of Bonsai Clubs International, for extending to me the hospitality of that organization and for allowing me to photograph many of their plants.

And deep, warm thanks are expressed to the many other club members and independent growers who permitted me to photograph the best possible bonsai—their own. Most generous were: Gaye Donaldson and Don Croxton of the American Bonsai Society;
  I. R. Bilskey, A. W. Blackhall, Mr. and Mrs. Paul Jodian, Harvey Olsen, Lu and Gil Pitman, Robert and Helen Woodward, and Remo Zaro of the East Bay Bonsai Club;

Dr. and Mrs. Francis E. Howard of the Kusamura Bonsai Club; Bob and Peggy Krohn of the Marin Bonsai Club; Barrie Coate of the Midori Bonsai Club; Mrs. Leonard W. Renick of the San Francisco Bonsai Club.

I am also grateful to: Dan Buckley, Max Cann, Henry Fukuchi, Mrs. Emil Steinegger, Pete Sugawara, and Ken Sugimoto.

The names of the owners of each bonsai or tray landscape appear in the captions under the photographs. Where no name is given, the bonsai are my own.

Contents

About Bonsai,
Saikei and Bonkei

The art of bonsai is neither new to gardening nor to the West. In 1843, Robert Fortune, an agent for the Royal Horticultural Society reported from China:

> The dwarfed trees of the Chinese and Japanese have been noticed by every author who has written upon these countries and all have attempted to give some description of the methods by which the effect is produced. The process is in reality a very simple one and is based upon one of the commonest principles of vegetable physiology. We all know that anything which retards in any way the free circulation of the sap, also prevents to a certain extent the formation of wood and leaves. This may be accomplished by grafting, by confining the roots, withholding water, bending the branches, or in a hundred other ways, which all proceed from the same principles. This is perfectly understood by the Chinese and they make nature subservient to this particular whim.[1]

These words still stand as a penetrating description of bonsai. But the Orient, Japan in particular, offered more in the way of miniature gardening than Robert Fortune found, for example, miniature landscapes called bonkei. And now there is a modern version of this known as saikei.

Bon means tray in Japanese. Thus a bonsai (bone-sigh) is a tray planting, and a bonkei (bone-kay) a tray scape, landscape or seascape. Saikei (sigh-kay), apparently a coined word, means much the

[1] Robert Fortune, *Three Years' Wanderings in the Northern Provinces of China*, Royal Horticultural Society, London, 1847.

9

same, the difference being that a bonkei is essentially a "dry" landscape, and living plants are seldom used; a saikei depends exclusively on living plants for effect.

Materials for the three are readily available. Plants for bonsai and saikei can come from your garden, a local nursery, or the wild. I buy *keto* clays for bonkei from Japanese shops, and several substitutes can also be used. Bonsai, bonkei, and saikei do have Oriental backgrounds, but I can see Occidental futures for them—and that is what this book is all about.

Magalia, California   Robert Lee Behme
January, 1969

Bonsai, Saikei and Bonkei

1. Bonsai— The Art and the Styles

When I came into the open above the timberline the white-capped peak of Mount Gibson was not far above. The few weathered trees were bright in the California sun and the blue sky was spotted with soft, white clouds. I hiked slowly up the slope, breathing hard against the altitude, and there it was, on the edge of a sharp precipice—a magnificent three-foot ponderosa pine, windswept and contorted, sustained by little more than a handful of earth.

The sight of that lone tree was something I did not forget It was an experience that gave me a new awareness of trees. As a photographer, I had always been interested in them, but before I had viewed them more as an aspect of the landscape than as exciting individual specimens. Now I began really to "see" trees and to "collect" them, that is to make a collection of photographs of them.

My travel kit always includes the American Forestry Association's list of the one hundred oldest and tallest trees, and tells me where to locate them. When a trip brings me past one, I take pictures.

One day my wife and I were driving through Logan Canyon in northern Utah when a sign pointing to the "Jardine Juniper" caught our attention. My list identified it as "The World's Oldest Living Western Red Juniper," so we hiked three miles up a steep trail to find the tree growing from a jutting rock. That tree was well worth the effort, and I photographed it from several angles. I've used pictures of its twisted, ancient branches to style several bonsai.

Then at Yosemite National Park last fall we hiked to the top of a rocky knoll to see the "Oldest Jeffrey Pine on Record," a specimen six centuries old. Wind, rain, and snow had created a form with great emotional impact. Again I shot many pictures of it.

NATURE, THE EXAMPLE

This interest in trees per se inevitably led me to an interest in bonsai, at first as an enthusiastic admirer, then, because I am a gardener, to the training of bonsai myself, and also to an interest in tray landscapes, replicas of memories my photographer's eye has so often enjoyed. This then is how I "came to bonsai."

I do not actually copy my pictures but the dramatic shapes I have recorded guide me in designing, and I have used ideas from that fascinating Jeffrey pine in four of my most successful bonsai.

If one English word applies to the Japanese concept of bonsai, that word is scale. Plants chosen for training might, in nature, grow to giant heights; but with roots confined, trees are kept small and every part—trunk, limbs, leaves, and the container that holds them—is scaled to give an impression of full size but in miniature. Beauty lies not only in the specimens themselves, but also in what they can suggest. Here we are inclined to be delighted by the specimens themselves; in Japan, it

This Jeffrey pine, *Pinus jeffreyi,* growing in Yosemite National Park, is estimated to be some six centuries old—a magnificent prototype for a bonsai.

is what they represent, their nostalgic and traditional associations, that are considered more significant than the plants themselves.

As bonsai become increasingly popular here, certain misconceptions arise. Recently, in Seattle I was asked, "Why do people grow those stunted, dwarfed trees?"

"Good bonsai are neither," I replied. "They are never undernourished, never intentionally grown to grotesque shapes. The art lies in maintaining health and size while training to natural forms."

That bonsai must be old is another erroneous idea. Some of the exquisite trees we see in shows or pictured in books are indeed old, but most of them only give an impression of age. So when I am asked, "Do I need old plants to grow bonsai?" my answer is that we overemphasize age. The life span of a bonsai is about the same as the life span of a species grown naturally. Only a few can be said to have impressive longevity. Most of the old trees we see are imported from Japan. Even there age is not revered at the expense of such significant features as fine form and attractive appearance. In this country, aside from some gnarled old plants collected from the wild, we have few ancient native bonsai. We simply haven't been collecting and training long enough. Some of the finest American bonsai here are really youngsters ten to twenty years old. Many have been in containers less than five years.

The training of bonsai probably originated before the eleventh century in China, where they were called *p'en tsai,* the precursor of the Japanese name. Very likely the dwarf trees were developed from small temple landscapes, like bonkei, that symbolized Horai-san, the sacred Taoist mountain of eternal youth, and the bonsai were the trees that grew on the steep slopes. Although there are other theories, thirteenth- and fourteenth-century scrolls picture temples with shallow boxes in the courtyards. Some of the boxes contain small trees; others, mounds of earth that suggest mountains.

At first, grotesque, deformed trees were considered good art. It was not until the mid-1800's that growers in Azakusa Park, a famous nursery center near Tokyo, coined the name bonsai and turned to nature for guidance in shaping their trees. The Emperor Meiji encouraged them, and by the twentieth century bonsai had become a national art of Japan.

The art came slowly to the West. One of the earliest exhibitions was held in London in 1909, and about the same time a grower from Yokohama, a Mr. Sato brought to New York the first bonsai most Americans had ever seen. Although Sato and the London show caused comment, neither did much to popularize bonsai. Sato held private exhibitions and sold many of his plants to wealthy New Yorkers, but steam heat

15

and lack of information on how to grow them soon caused their demise. Thus the myth arose that bonsai belong to Japan and are not suited to our conditions—or to our attitudes.

Gardeners, experienced ones at that, still tell me, "I can't grow bonsai. You have to think as a Japanese to do it." But I soon discover most of them have never tried. They seem to think the techniques as both difficult and mysterious.

This is far from the truth. If you can grow other potted plants you can learn to grow bonsai, and you don't need an Oriental turn of mind to be successful. Bonsai offer delightful contrast to full-scale gardening, a solution to problems of space, an elegant, artistic form of expression. Culture is not complicated. Just as confined conditions and natural elements keep some wild trees small, certain cultural techniques, purposely applied, accomplish the same thing for our plants.

Dwarfing depends upon growing in a minimal amount of soil, fast drainage, planned prunings, and sometimes wiring. Because objectives differ from those for other container-grown plants, bonsai are watered, fertilized, top- and root-pruned differently. A house plant is rarely repotted until it is root-bound. Bonsai are repotted and root-pruned on schedule to keep them both small and healthy.

Culture is not complicated, but when I began a friend exclaimed with horror, "You'll lose your mind. There's so much to learn and it takes forever."

He was wrong. While bonsai is hardly one-season gardening from a packet, it is neither so complex nor so prolonged as my friend imagined. Techniques are fun to learn and the technical jargon, not difficult to master. I discovered it was possible to develop attractive bonsai in a year or two if that was my objective, and in the beginning it was. I made "instant" bonsai, pruning, trimming, and potting low-growing shrubs, like juniper with immediate and pleasing results.

Some people call bonsai-growing an art, others call it a hobby. I believe it can be both, the difference more a matter of plant perfection than personal attitude. I find a special green-thumb enjoyment in growing bonsai, in training and trimming plants. No other type of gardening has proved so enjoyable.

It is safe to say that every month hundreds are attempting bonsai for the first time. There is an international society, Bonsai Clubs International, firmly established on the West Coast and the American Bonsai Society has been formed in New York. Both societies have national boards and yearly conventions. The Brooklyn Botanic Garden, one of the first bonsai centers in this country, has offered classes in culture and techniques for years, and registration has steadily increased. In many large cities major shows and demonstrations are held each year, and the attendance is astounding. An exhibition in one city drew more than

2,000 spectators over one weekend. The same is true in smaller places. Admittedly, bonsai-growing will hardly become our most popular garden art—and some enthusiasts say they like its exclusive "in" quality—but many predict that memberships and interest will triple in the coming decade.

In Japan several "schools" have developed, each with its own techniques. The master of one insists on a complex soil mixture for certain deciduous trees; another master recommends a very different mixture for the same trees. The fact that both techniques are successful proves only one point; there is more leeway in the culture of bonsai than is generally admitted.

One enthusiast remarked, "There is only one way to describe bonsai—small, smaller, smallest." In the interest of simplicity his idea has merit, but as bonsai became popular in Japan, growers devised a more complicated system. They classified plants by size, growing angle, styling, and the number of plants in one container. Now there are some thirty recognized divisions and sub-divisions.

Dedicated growers familiarize themselves with all of them and learn the Japanese terminology as well. For ready reference, I have made a simplified chart, an easier procedure since many of the categories are flexible, and furthermore, bonsai are artistic creations that often defy a stylized label.

Classification by Size

Category	Description	Height
Mame	(Mah-may, "little bean"). Smallest, raised from seeds, seedlings, and cuttings since even tiny plants are effective; considered most difficult size to maintain, often shifted on to become full-sized bonsai.	Fingertip to 6 inches.
Ko	(Koh). Small bonsai, one of the two most common sizes, young plants often in this category, can be held as *ko* for years.	7 to 11 inches.
Chui	(Chew-ey). Medium size, almost any bonsai can be held to this size.	12 to 24 inches.
Dai	(Digh). Largest, used for garden planters, often collected almost full-grown from the wild.	24 to more than 36 inches, the average less than 33 inches.

Growing angle Category	Description	Container
Upright	Duplicates the most usual natural angle, vertical from the ground, at right angles to container; subdivisions of formal and informal.	Shallow—rectangular, oval, octagonal, circular.
Slanting	Trunk curved or straight, at an angle to container; branches on all sides of trunk.	Rectangular and oval, shallow to accommodate the "reach" of the plant.
Windswept	Similar to slanting style, but branches in only one direction, as if wind-blown.	Shallow—rectangular usually best; ovals for a few designs.
Cascade	Trunk and branches sweep out and below top of container, often below its base; rarely much height to plant; lower branches create important aspect of the design.	Deep, to balance design and emphasize the unusual form.

Styling	Description	Container
Formal	Generally upright, trunk straight; branches symmetrical, well spaced, tapering toward tip; uppermost part of trunk with great vitality, except for dead—"snag" or *jin*—tips, which become part of design.	Shallow, many kinds.
Informal	Upright, with one trunk in gentle S-curve less pronounced near tip.	Shallow, rectangular, or oval.
Roots-out-of-ground	Tree with unusual root growth visible above ground as part of design.	Shallow, shape depending on styling; size and design chosen to set off roots.
With rocks	Growing over rocks, from rocks, leaning against rocks, etc.	Shallow, oval or rectangular to support height.

Classification by Style

Multiple plantings	Description	Container
With single trees	Styling as for other single trees, but several planted together.	Shallow oval or rectangular depending on size of grouping.
With twin-trunks or double trees	Two-trunk tree, growing from one root; fork visible; one trunk always smaller than the other; balance of trunk sizes and angles important.	Usually shallow, the growing angle dictating the shape.
With root-connected trunks	"Forest" grouping; multiple-trunk plantings composed of a number of single-trunk trees, root connected; or from one root planted horizontally, at or below ground-level, the upright branches becoming trunks in *ikada* or "raft" style.	Circular and oval for tight growth patterns; long and rectangular when growth is spread out.
Multiple trunks, not connected, grove or group plantings.	Usually with trees of one species, although related species may be combined for contrast; but rarely deciduous with evergreens.	Shallow, long rectangular; sometimes a rock serves as container.

Enormous surface roots of this ancient pine follow rock crevices and suggest a way to reveal roots on a bonsai.

This lodgepole pine, a windswept bonsai—a form similar to slanting styles—does indeed appear to be blown by a strong gale. Placement to the side of the wooden container and the anchoring rock contribute to the effect. Lu and Gil Pitman.

Nature is rich in bonsai forms like this Jeffrey pine in Yosemite National Park.

This Japanese white pine, *Pinus parviflora*, is one of the trees imported by the late Larz Anderson, U.S. Ambassador to Japan in the early 1900's, and displayed at the Arnold Arboretum in Massachusetts. The form suggests that of the Jeffrey pine in the preceding photograph.

We found this "Jardine Juniper, the Oldest Living Western Red Juniper," after a three-mile hike up a Utah mountainside. Bonsai with branches of dead wood or *jin* are inspired by such specimens.

23

Collected high on western mountains, this bonsai of juniper retains a "snag" or *jin* tip, dead wood, as weather-beaten trees often do in nature. Connie and Horace Hinds.

Age has been overemphasized in bonsai culture. (*Above*), A Japanese boxwood, container-grown for only seven years by Bob and Peggy Krohn, already has the look of age, and compares favorably with the century-old cypress, *Chamaecyparis obtusa* (below), at the Arnold Arboretum.

Deadwood is an effective aspect of this Japanese five-needle pine. Dan Buckley.

Ken Sugimoto, a professional bonsai-grower from Palo Alto, California, gives a demonstration, sponsored by the Peninsula Bonsai Club, on the front lawn of a Buddhist church.

A collection of *mame*—the smallest of all bonsai forms and not exceeding six inches—
displayed at a show of the American Bonsai Society.

This 150-year-old cypress, *Chamaecyparis obtusa,* with a marvelously gnarled trunk, is part of the great bonsai collection at the Arnold Arboretum.

A five-inch cotoneaster, grown in the difficult *mame* form, stands beside a fifteen-inch, or medium-sized, *chui* bonsai, a tea-tree to indicate the comparative heights. Barrie Coate.

Dai bonsai may be grown up to three feet. Here a well-developed ponderosa pine in a heavy bronze bowl makes a handsome garden accent. Peter Ioka.

A thirty-year-old imported Chinese elm in upright styling duplicates the most common growing angle of trees in nature. Upright bonsai are also classified as formal and informal. Peter Ioka.

A good cascade sweeps out and below the container, as does this *Juniperus procumbens,* displayed on a stand. Gaye Donaldson.

Cascades are often potted so their branches can extend below the container. This Japanese black pine is set high upon a heavy section of root, a natural pedestal, compatible with bonsai. Henry Matsutani.

Japanese black pine, an informal upright bonsai, features a gentle S-curve. Shallow, rectangular, or oval containers are excellent for this style. Yoshio Sato.

(*Above left*), An ikada or raft is created from a dwarf Reeves tea-tree grown on its side, the branches on the upper edge developing as trunks. Barrie Coate. (*Right*), Roots of this plum above ground contribute drama to the design. Yoshio Sato. (*Below left*), Thirty-year-old zelkova trained in upright style by K. Murata. Owners, Bob and Peggy Krohn. (*Right*), Hawthorn with multiple trunks, a difficult style. Gaye Donaldson.

36

An Hinoki cypress in twin-trunk style, the larger trunk representing the parent, the smaller, the child is most effective because of the sharpness of the V and the balance between the size of the trunks. Peter Ioka.

2. Plants—How to Buy and Develop Them

In time, usually a very short time, beginners become collectors with twelve to twenty trees. Soon they may have more than a hundred, and dedicated growers, three times that number. But if you are prone to quantity, keep in mind that big collections are demanding. Try—but who is successful?—to assemble only as many plants as you can comfortably care for.

I know enthusiasts who want one of every important type, others who specialize, as in azaleas, or only in trees collected from the wild. A collector of deciduous varieties says, "They provide an exciting display of everything plants can offer—flowers, fruit, and autumn color. Why bother with evergreens; to me they look static."

However, my own collection leans heavily upon these, especially on conifers, although it includes trident and Japanese maples, and a few flowering and fruiting trees. I prefer such an array to plants of just one type.

SELECTING YOUR FIRST PLANTS

If you want to start with mature trees, buy them trained or partially trained from collectors and professional nurserymen. In time your collection will probably consist mainly of home-started or home-trained bonsai. But bonsai beyond first stages are more encouraging, and offer a ready means of finding out about culture.

When you are looking for plants, watch for untrained trees with well-developed trunks, sturdy, well-spaced, interesting branches and leaves or needles in good scale. These become better-than-average bonsai. Minor growth voids are not cause for rejection but unhealthy branches are. These may require recuperative repairs, sometimes called hospi-

Beginners soon become collectors with twelve to twenty trees, and some accumulate hundreds. John A. Dutro.

talization, and hospitalization needs an expert touch. In a word, let structure be your important guide.

With few exceptions, dense foliage and symmetrical limbs are not essentials. Often trees with less foliage and asymmetrical branch structures are more interesting. Years ago I discovered a trick that makes it easier to pick prospects. I evaluate trees from the side that offers the most interesting view of the trunk; this would become the front. The front may not be obvious on an untrained tree; in fact it may not even be visible until I mentally trim away branches, but it is the place from which good bonsai evolve.

To set the tone, I look for a branch at one third the height; some growers require two branches. The low branch, or branches, should be sturdy; I may want to train one to the side or toward the back to add depth. A weak branch might die under training and then the tree would lose character.

If I had to limit purchases to one source that source would be a local nursery. Large cities offer the conventional commercial outlet with a variety of garden plants but there are also specialized bonsai nurseries.

To start a collection with mature trees, buy them ready-trained from professional growers. This two-century-old azalea is an expensive example. Trained in Japan and imported by Ken Sugimoto, its price, $2,500.

Off-balance trees like this Japanese black pine are often the most interesting. The trick in selecting likely prospects is to evaluate them for a good front view, the place from which the design will evolve. Henry Fukuchi.

Specialists are more common than you may think. In the San Francisco suburbs, I found seven well-stocked bonsai nurseries in one day. A shopping center in another city offered bonsai in its garden shop. Once, on a drive through a remote section of Arizona, I discovered a bonsai nursery beside the highway.

The number of sources is increasing but the general nursery remains your consistent supplier. A well-stocked one offers plants in various stages of development, and you can select at the best time for transplanting, pruning, or wiring. You choose from four kinds of stock:

Liner plants are young production-line stock developed from seeds and cuttings. In an earlier time they were set out in lines or rows to mature. Now most of them are grown in flats or individual containers. Little labor is involved and so they are cheap to produce. Seedlings generally have a better root system than cuttings. You can buy two, three, or more for a dollar—young, supple, easily-shaped trees, excellent for *mame* (tiny bonsai), grove, and forest plantings. The most promising can be developed into large single bonsai.

Container plants in the West, at least, are sold in tin or plastic cans. The youngest are about twice the age of liners, the oldest may be much older. Most of these are well suited to *ko* or small bonsai. Plants in one- and five-gallon cans may be used for *chui* or even *dai* sizes. Most of my bonsai have been container plants, and I always search the stock thoroughly.

Plants in small cans or pots have shallow roots, and when the season is right, they can be set directly in bonsai containers. Plants with larger, more complex root systems are better transplanted in two steps. Cut the roots by one-third, and plant in a large clay training pot. The second year, root-prune again and transplant to a smaller container. Two-stage transplanting reduces shock and results in a healthier plant.

Bare-root plants are sold heavily pruned, without soil, and only during the dormant season. Stock is limited to deciduous species. Most of it will be leggier than good form demands, but useful plants can be discovered. Since bare-root stock is heavily pruned, it is excellent for grafting.

Balled-and-burlapped plants, "B & B" are good prospects. Difficult-to-transplant stock, trees collected from the wild, and certain species of broad-leafs and conifers are sold this way with root systems intact and protected by a burlap wrapping. Since these are among the easiest to transplant, they are great for beginners.

43

(*Left*), A liner, like this cryptomeria, is a young production-line nursery plant, usually a bargain. Seedlings generally have better root systems than cuttings. (*Above*), Plants are often sold in cans, young ones may be two to three years old, older ones up to seven years. Good bonsai can be developed from container plants, like this bristlecone pine (*far left*), a specimen of the oldest living species. Gaye Donaldson.

Nurseries usually throw misshapen trees and shrubs in discard piles. This material is not suited to conventional gardening but sometimes the very best bonsai material is here, and it can be purchased at bargain prices.

While nursery stock will account for most of your plants, there are other sources. If you are adventurous—and lucky—you will locate some plants in the wild. However, you will eventually want kinds you can only obtain from seeds, cuttings, or layerings.

Bonsai from Seed

Seed-grown trees take time, but if you raise them in flats they are stronger than trees you can collect. Seedlings develop better root systems—shallow with a good spread. Taproot development is limited and may not occur. Some plants, zelkova is one, produce thicker, more symmetrical growth from seed. Seedlings make excellent *mame,* and are also good for grove plantings. If you have a penchant for rare species, seed may be the way to get them. Some kinds can be imported no other way.

WHERE TO OBTAIN

You can collect your own seeds but it is a tedious business. I have never tried, but Kay Craig, a bonsai-grower in Arizona, regularly sends collected seeds to members of bonsai clubs around the world. I've grown her seeds with success. If you are the patient type, collect seeds from a healthy parent tree. If you plan to mail seeds, be sure the tree has been free of whitefly, spider mites, and aphids—all carriers of virus.

You can buy seeds from several sources. In the East, seedsmen offer a good selection from native trees, and imported varieties as well. West-Coast growers list most of the Western natives. You can order foreign seeds direct from growers abroad. One Japanese catalogue lists more than a hundred species including nine varieties of fir (*Abies*) and one of jujube (*Zizyphus*). Prices range from one to five dollars a pound. A Danish catalogue lists twenty species of fir, including varieties from Russia, Korea, and Denmark, plus thirty-seven pines and fifty others including ginkgo, larch, and cotoneaster.

Most plants can be raised from seed but these kinds are the easiest: beech, birch, fir, ginkgo, hornbeam, larch, liquidambar (sweetgum), maple, pine, pomegranate, spruce, and yew.

HOW TO SOW

Sow seeds early in spring in shallow bulb pots, bonsai containers, or flats. I prefer flats; they are inexpensive and convenient. The standard size here is 14½-by-23-by-3 inches—a little larger than the Japanese type. Although our size is practical, a full flat can be heavy—thirty-five pounds when filled with moist earth. Women prefer the half-flat, which can be either 12-by-12 or 12-by-18 inches, and a half-flat can be soaked in a laundry tub.

45

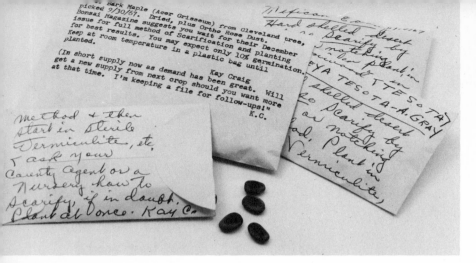

(*Above left*), Seed packets sent by an enthusiast to bonsai club members around the world. (*Right*), Flats, full or half size are easy to use; drilled holes or full-length slits are essential for drainage. (*Below left*), Some seeds need scarification, as here against medium-grit sandpaper. (*Right*), Vermiculite provides a fast-draining, sterile medium. Peat cups are convenient, one seed to each cup. (*Bottom*), Cups are placed over a layer of sand in a flat. Water the flat, if you haven't done it before.

(*Above left*), Seedlings like this three-year-old coastal redwood make good bonsai. Dr. and Mrs. Francis E. Howard. (*Above right*), Cuttings are a good way to propagate important plants. (*Below*), Air-layering on this juniper is a method of rooting above ground in moss wrapped with plastic. Gaye Donaldson.

If you plant in used containers, first clean them well. Wash clay pots in hot soapy water with a couple of tablespoons of household bleach added. Scrub, then rinse thoroughly. Clean wood flats with a stiff brush dipped in hot suds; protect the inside with a copper-based paint, which also disinfects. Avoid creosote, which is harmful to many plants.

Provide good drainage. Clay pots should have at least one one-inch hole; flats, either full-length slits or several three-quarter-inch holes. You can plant directly in a container or in peat pots set in a flat.

For most seeds a good soil mixture consists of equal parts of sand and loam; a few species like zelkova do better with less sand. If you have a tendency to overwater, as I sometimes do, add a little more sand to facilitate drainage. Spruce and yew do better in this sandier mix.

Screen the soil reasonably fine and, preferably, disinfect it. Or plant in vermiculite, which comes sterilized and provides a fast-draining medium.

Some seeds need stratification or scarification. Commercial seeds carry instructions. Even when seeds do not need special preparation, I soak them twelve hours before I sow. Soaking helps separate the fertile from the infertile. Fertile seeds sink. I scrape off and discard those that float.

When you hand-plant seeds, put them singly in peat pots, or one-half to one inch apart in rows. Then they will be easy to prick out. Fine seeds can be sown uncovered or given just a sprinkling of sand. Cover large seeds in flats with a thin layer of soil, in peat pots with vermiculite.

HOW TO WATER

The best way to water is a controversial subject. Some growers water after preparing the flat but before sowing, by soaking the flat, up to the rim, for a few minutes. They claim that watering at this point avoids the danger of disturbing the seeds. Others prefer to water with a fine rose after seeding, but watering then can wash the seeds. I soak flats, either before or after seeding; soaking does not disturb surface sowings. After you water the flat, cover it with newspaper and a sheet of glass, or with two papers and a sheet of plastic, or three newspapers alone.

Set flats in a warm place, away from direct sun. A lath house is ideal. Keep the soil moist and avoid temperature variations. Remove the glass or plastic once a day, wipe off moisture, then replace. When signs of germination appear, usually two to three weeks after planting, discard the paper and prop up one end of the glass. Remove the glass after another week.

Bonsai from Cuttings

Bonsai may not grow from cuttings with the ease of a geranium, but cuttings are a good way to propagate important plants. Try these first: azalea, flowering quince, forsythia, olive, poplar, rhododendron, spruce, tamarisk, willow, and wisteria.

Cuttings take less time than seeds. Many growers favor them for *mame* and *ko* bonsai. You can use discarded prunings from rare and expensive trees. With cuttings, variety and color always come true. However, cuttings may not develop the spreading root system you get with seedlings, a fact that makes cuttings undesirable for rock-grown bonsai.

Make softwood cuttings in spring; hardwoods later, in some cases not till fall. Take softwood cuttings from new growth only; hardwood cuttings should include new growth and a heel of old wood. In either case, cut from terminal or tip growth or from the end of a healthy side shoot. The quality of the material has a direct effect on the development of the plant. Good cuttings are more likely to root even under poor conditions. Avoid weak, coarse shoots. They generally form poor root systems and are often subject to disease.

Make cuttings with a downward slant. A beveled cut lessens the danger of rot. Some growers make a second, shallower cut just below the lowest leaf node to improve the moisture intake. Many swear by root hormones; I know one who claims the only cuttings that root for her are those so treated. Others find that hormones neither help nor harm plants. A few consider that rooting powders delay propagation. But, in general, evidence seems to favor the use of hormones. I dip cuttings according to the manufacturer's directions; then insert about two thirds their length in the prepared soil.

Mist flats of cuttings two or three times a day for the first week; then gradually decrease the schedule. In extremely dry areas, you can reduce moisture loss by covering flats with plastic. If you do, lift the cover at least three times a week to insure circulation of air. Keep the flat in a shady place for two to three weeks; then gradually expose to the sun. Increase the interval until, at the end of about two months, plants are receiving a normal amount of sun for the species.

Bonsai from Layering

Layering is a means of developing a second set of roots on a growing plant. In a way, it is similar to rooting by cutting, but layering can be done either above or below ground. The difference is that the section being rooted receives some nourishment from the parent—but not complete nourishment. Therefore it develops roots as a secondary source of food.

There are two kinds of layering: ground-layering, familiar to most Americans, and air-layering, a more difficult technique developed centuries ago in China. Both are good ways to develop new trees without damage to mature plants. You can select the point at which new roots will appear, and utilize the branches above that point for a second bonsai.

Air-layering also offers a way to shorten leggy trees. When new roots develop on the trunk at the proper height, you can discard the old trunk and roots. Many growers side-step layering because it takes time. Deciduous trees may root in six months; evergreens can take two years or more. Deciduous trees should be layered in spring before buds appear.

Easy plants to propagate by ground- or air-layering include: beech, birch, crape-myrtle, cryptomeria, camellia, juniper, maple, pine, spruce, and willow.

Ground-layering Softwoods like juniper can be ground-layered with almost certain success. Bend a selected branch to the ground, and make a small cut on the underside. Insert a stone in the cut to keep it open. Then remove leaves from the area, and bury the stripped part of the branch under four inches of soil. Support the leafy end above ground with a stake. Keep the soil moist. Softwoods may root in as little as six weeks.

Hardwoods are rarely worth ground-layering. Most of them have to be buried deep, packed with moss, and kept moist for a long time. Some will not root in less than three years; for these, there are faster ways of propagation.

Air-layering Pines and birches are among the plants considered ideal for air-layering. The limiting factor is size. Generally a four-year-old branch or trunk is best, one about one and one-half inches in diameter, although experts consider anything up to two inches "easy." Thicker branches and trunks usually require special treatment since protective callousing may cause a wound to heal without developing roots.

Girdle an evergreen with a thin copper wire at the place where you wish new roots to form. The wire acts like a tourniquet, drastically reducing the flow of sap and so forcing the section above to grow roots for survival. I use 20-gauge wire.

Wrap the girdled area with moistened sphagnum moss, then cover it with plastic. Some growers tie the plastic or fasten the ends with rubber bands. Others make perforations in the wrap and leave the top open. Either system works so long as the moss is kept damp. Excessive moisture can act as an evaporative cooler, retarding rooting.

Cut the bark on deciduous trees around the rooting circle. Slice through the cambium layer in a ring twice the diameter of branch or trunk; then "dish" the woody material below toward the center. Don't make it thin or wood may break. Many trees root better when you girdle the top of the cut as well, perhaps with a piece of twine. Cover the wound with sphagnum moss, then wrap with plastic.

After the new roots develop, cut away the grafted section from the parent. Remove the plastic, and pot immediately without disturbing the moss. Keep the plant moist and shaded for two to three weeks, then gradually expose to the sun.

Bonsai by Grafting

The process of joining parts of two plants so that they grow as one, is valuable. In Japan, *horai*-style bonsai are developed from white pine grafted to black or red pine. Brocade pine is usually grown on black-pine stock. As I travel, I see more and more Americans attempting to graft bonsai. At one midwestern nursery nearly half of the trees I admired had been developed from grafts.

Grafting gives you an edge. It lets you improve an imperfect bonsai. You can add branches, reduce the height of a leggy tree, save one condemned to death by root damage, or get more than one flower color on a single trunk. If you want to try grafting, begin with these easy trees: ginkgo, maple, holly, and pine, especially Japanese varieties, such as white and black.

A graft requires two parts: the rooted plant or stock, and a cutting or scion—the word means child or descendant. Make a cut in the stock and insert the scion in the cut. The parts will grow together yet retain individuality. Recently, in California, at the University Nursery in Berkeley owned by Yoshio Sato, I saw a beautiful quince grafted to carry flowers of red, white, and pink.

Some growers avoid grafting because of tradition. It was once out of favor because the union between stock and scion invariably produced unsightly swollen growth. Better techniques, with smaller cuts and tapered scions, avoid this.

Top and side grafts are most common. For a *top graft* the foliage and upper limb structure are removed (usually at the trunk, although important branches and forks can remain). The stock, with roots, is then less than a foot high. The purpose of a top graft is to create a new branch structure. A *side graft*, made lower on the trunk, is designed to fill a void with an extra branch.

I learned grafting from Mr. Sato. He makes grafts early in spring, when buds are dormant and sap has just begun to flow. Scions are selected in advance; Sato uses only strong tips. Normally they are two or three inches long, although longer ones are sometimes used as side grafts. They are kept in a clean jar to minimize the chance of disease.

Sato says, "A successful graft depends on speed and cleanliness. Sap from stock and scion must bind for cells to unite. It is important to expose cut areas for the shortest possible time." He prepares everything in advance—stock, scions, tools—placing them on a bench where all is kept scrupulously clean. "If you have any doubts about cleanliness, sterilize tools," he urges.

Smooth the top of the trunk with a knife. This is essential to reduce the danger of rot and disease. If a trunk is more than one inch across, puncture it about half an inch deep between the wood and cambium layers, rather than making a conventional wedge-cut. "Union between stock and scion will then be less obvious," Sato would explain.

HOW TO TOP-GRAFT

Trim the scion to a paper-thin taper. Insert it into the puncture as far as it will go without separating or damaging bark. This way up to three scions can be grafted to one trunk.

When stock is thinner than one inch, make a wedge-cut one inch deep, through the center and parallel with the trunk. Insert the scion on the edge, at the cambium layer. Two scions can be grafted at once, one on each edge.

Wrap the stock to hold parts firmly. Thread or vinyl tape will work, although Sato prefers rubber because "elasticity holds without marks." Cover areas exposed by the graft with a protective tree-paint. Local nurseries usually have several good compounds. Most of them dissolve and disappear within a year.

Place the grafted stock in a training bed, protecting it with a glass jar. When buds become active, remove the glass, and the plant will grow normally. After one growing season, you can transplant to a pot. Remove wrappings after one year if they have not fallen free.

HOW TO SIDE-GRAFT

In side-grafting, treat stock the same as in top-grafting. Clean the roots; then make a gentle, angled cut one to two inches long on the trunk. Cut through the cambium layer, but don't go deeper. For the sake of the future design, make the cut low on the trunk, at ground-level if possible. In time the graft can be hidden by soil.

Instead of cutting the scion with equal-length tapers, keep one side shorter. Place the short side up, against the trunk; this will give the scion a natural growing angle. Only one scion can be grafted to a cut. Wrap the parts; then protect with grafting compound. Plant as you would other stock.

(Budding is a technique that grafts a bud instead of a cutting. Insert the bud between the wood and cambium layers to produce a new limb. The advantage of budding is that it leaves a smaller scar. Usually budding is reserved for the few delicate trees whose bark peels readily, such as cherry and peach. Budding is a difficult, risky operation.)

(*Above left*), Yoshio Sato makes a wedge-cut for top-grafting. (*Right*), The tapered scion is inserted in the stock. (*Lower left*), When the trunk is less than in inch thick, a wedge-cut is used. (*Right*), The cut is made one to one and one-half inches deep to insure a bond between stock and scion.

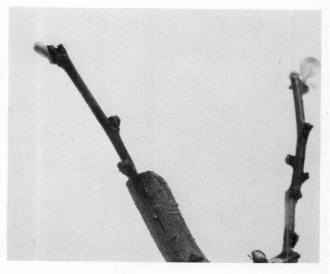

(*Above*), String should be firm, not tight enough to girdle. (*Below*), Wrapping limits movement until cells of the two parts grow together.

Only two scions are grafted to one wedge cut on each side of the stock since cambium layers must touch to grow. Here stock has grafts on each side of this.

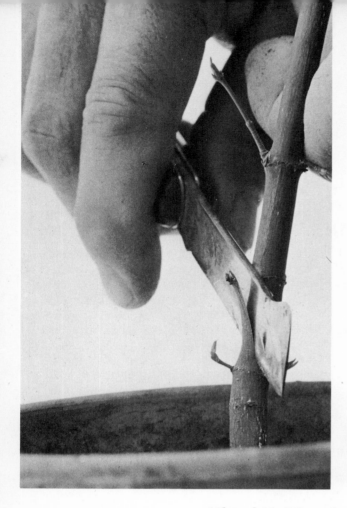
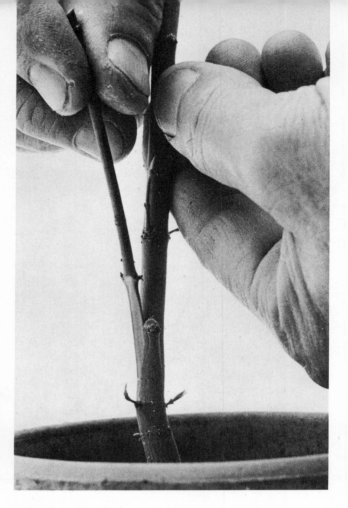

(*Above left*), Side graft can add a branch. The cut is made low so the graft can be hidden as the tree grows. (*Right*), The scion is cut with an unequal taper. (*Lower left*), The short side of the taper lies against the tree, to give the scion a natural growing angle. (*Right*), Stock and scion are firmly wrapped with thread or vinyl tape, but preferably rubber.

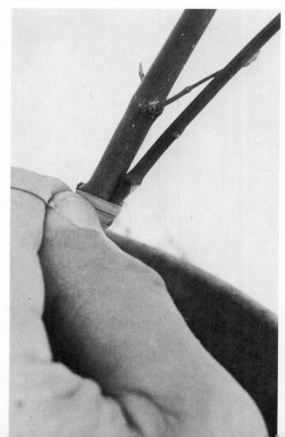

(*Above left*), Scions are cut early in spring, and placed in a sterile container. (*Right*), The area for a graft should be clean and smooth to reduce danger of rot. (*Lower left*), On thick trunks a small puncture is made one-half to one inch deep between cambium and wood. (*Right*), Three scions can be used to a stock with the puncture technique.

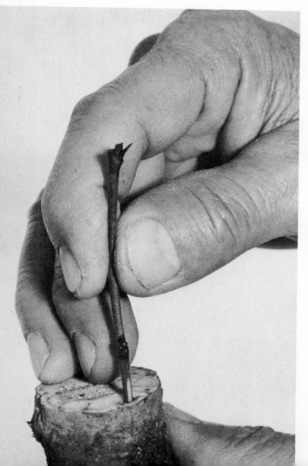

(*Above*), Grafted stock is set under glass in a training bed. (*Below*), Graft plants are transplanted to containers after one or two years; string or rubber wrappings removed.

Collecting is a most enjoyable way to find new stock. If you like week-end rambles or Sunday drives in the country, you are well on your way to collecting. Some of my most impressive plants have been discovered in high country behind my house. Other fine plants have come from abandoned farms and orchards at lower elevations.

I set out with a shovel, ax, twine, burlap sacks, and plastic bags, if possible also a jug of water. With such equipment, I can transplant any tree. Even when I return empty handed, and many trips do end this way, I've had fun. I've observed how different trees grow, and this knowledge helps me to design better bonsai. When I find a usable tree, it is like discovering gold.

Collecting can be done at any time during the growing season, but chances of success are best as plants come to the end of their dormant period. The spurt of new growth then carries a plant through the shock of transplanting. In mild climates, you can safely collect from the end of February to mid-April. In cold regions, May and June are better. Suprisingly, desert plants can be collected in the hottest summer months. Most species go dormant or semidormant then, to minimize the effects of the sun.

Clean the soil from around your trophy at least as far out as the spread of the foliage. The root system extends that far, often farther. Some collectors make a smaller circle, only about three times the trunk diameter, but I feel safer with a larger area. Dig a circular trench at the outer edge of the cleaned area with straight-sided cuts right through any roots there. For large, tough roots, you may need to use your ax.

You can unearth a tree in one day if time is a factor but chances of success are greater when you do the job in stages. I excavate one third of the roots first. Then I moisten them and repack the trench. On my second visit, sometimes a year later, I excavate deeper, changing from a straight-walled trench to one angled toward the center. Now I cut all roots except the taproot. On my third trip, three to six months later, I cut the taproot with an ax or a saw and remove the tree.

When the tree is free I moisten the root-ball, wrap it quickly with burlap, then put the whole thing—root-ball, trunk, and foliage—in a large plastic bag. The plastic provides a safe humid environment that immensely increases chances of success. At home I recut the taproot on a downward angle to reduce the possibility of root rot; then I plant the tree in my growing bed. I water it often the first week, misting the leaves daily to check transpiration. I protect the tree from sun and wind for a month, then gradually acclimate it.

HOW TO DIG,
TRANSPORT, AND SET OUT
A WILD PLANT

This river or white alder was collected rooted to the stump.

During the second growing year, I lift the plant, shorten roots, pot it, and commence training. If the root system is exceptionally large, I reduce the size over a longer period.

Don't collect indiscriminately from the wild. Without a special permit plants cannot be dug in national parks and forests, and remember that "wild" land in the mountains is privately owned. Get permission before you remove a tree.

There are many ways to collect legitimately. Bonsai clubs can obtain permission from state and federal foresters. Timber companies, who own some of the finest land in the West, are pleased to let collectors in. The best bonsai possibilities have little commercial value. I've often collected from Diamond National timber lands; the local offices quickly give me permission. In some areas, Arizona is one, organized tours take groups to high bonsai country. Rates are reasonable and experienced guides are on hand to help.

Almost any plant can be developed into a bonsai. At the end of this book is a chart suggesting more than fifty species (and nearly one hundred varieties) of the best possibilities. All are available in the United States. Some can be collected from the wild, others bought from local nurseries, a few only from bonsai specialists or nurseries specializing in American natives. Those marked with a star (*) are recommended for beginners.

Note: Growers with a deep concern for traditional Japanese goals may not agree with all of these selections. Their feeling is that "bonsai hold a mirror up to nature," which means that small trees are traditionally styled to the natural designs of their larger brothers. Shrubs, therefore, are not made into bonsai: they have no treelike counterparts. As one grower explained, "To use a shrub, it must be made into a copy of a tree."

I can hardly accept that concept for America. Fine bonsai can be made from such shrubs as cotoneaster, pyracantha, and viburnum, and their beauty gives them reason enough for being. If there is a drawback to native shrubs, it is that some are short-lived but the term is relative. It should not deter you from trying any that interest you.

An impressive thirty-five to fifty-year-old lodgepole pine was collected from high country.
Bob and Peggy Krohn.

3. Instant Bonsai

Your interest in bonsai presupposes an awareness of trees in nature. Perhaps on a trip you have been overwhelmed by the beauty of trees on a mountain top like this colony of fir with one ancient specimen towering splendidly above the rest. Or the trees on your lawn—which you have kept so meticulously pruned—may suggest bonsai designs to you. These zelkovas could later be the prototype for a group planting; this handsome weeping peach a model for a flowering bonsai. Perhaps a bonsai you have admired at a show or a picture seen in a book will be your inspiration. Here, as in Japan, the trend is toward a natural look, and form is best dictated by structure. Keep to simple designs; they nearly always work out best.

For your first attempt, why not try an "instant" bonsai? Make just one, and you will see how three bonsai techniques fit together. In less than an hour you can learn basic pruning, styling, and potting. Such a fast approach is certainly American, not Japanese, yet your first tree will be authentic in style.

Select a sturdy plant from a nursery, and buy one in a container. The root system will then be confined, partially trained, and easier to prune. For demonstrations, I often select a pine or juniper, and you will find either easy to work with. Of course, you could choose pyracantha or any of several other hardy shrubs. Be sure the plant you select is tough and fast-growing, a combination that helps it withstand the shock of concentrated "instant" pruning.

Prune your plant in its container if this seems easier. Later you may wish to remove trees before cutting so as to have a better view of the relationship between trunk and branches. This is less clearly seen over the rim of a pot or can. But with your first tree, it may be better if you keep techniques simple. Once plants are removed from their containers, roots are exposed and you must be concerned with keeping them moist.

A grove of spruce seen on a trip could be photographed for future reference. Dramatic forms can be helpful as you design bonsai.

1. The California juniper is an excellent source of material and makes a handsome bonsai. John Naka. Richard Gross photo.

2. *This variegated Camellia japonica, 'Finlandia', proves that camellias, properly handled, can make beautiful bonsai even though blooms and leaves are oversized Y. Sato.*

(*Above*), No bonsai is a copy of a full-grown tree though it helps to study trees. Zelkovas on a lawn could be a pattern for a grove bonsai. (*Below*), This flowering peach would look beautiful in miniature.

Before you do any pruning consider the possibilities of the plant you have chosen. Separate the foliage to determine the importance of each limb. Take time to decide which branches are essential to your design and which are not. Try to develop a "feel" for structure. If the tree is bushy, start by removing unimportant branches to expose the trunk— a key element in your styling. Next remove crossed branches and any weaker ones that would probably die.

As you work, check the importance of each limb by blocking it with your hand. If the design remains strong and vital with the branch blocked out, you know that branch can be removed. But be slow to remove deadwood, especially on conifers, until you are convinced it can be spared. Old, bleached wood called *jin* often adds character to a bonsai.

As you proceed, bend branches in different directions to see how changed lines affect styling. The idea is to organize branches into interesting groups. Traditional Japanese stylists rely on uneven elements —three, five, and seven, for example—yet rules are not so important as individual expression. If you are adventurous, create a design that appeals to you, regardless of rules. If, to begin with, you prefer the security of working by the book, keep in mind that classical proportions are based on thirds. The lowest third of the trunk is kept clear to show its relationship to soil and ground-cover. Let the central third be dominated by the main branches artistically spaced to reveal and emphasize the trunk. The top third of your bonsai should consist of fine, young branches and a tapering, active tip.

You can prune with a sharp knife, a razor blade, even your garden pruners, but the work goes better with shears and later you will probably want special bonsai shears. Whatever your tool, make close downward cuts that will produce smaller scars and direct water away from the wound and so help to prevent rot.

ROOT-PRUNING Once your instant bonsai is styled, remove it from the container, if you have not already done so, and proceed with root-pruning and potting, as the photographs indicate. Soils for bonsai are a study in themselves and at this point can wait. Use any good sandy loam. Later, when your bonsai is established and in need of repotting, you can change mixtures if a change is required.

Root-pruning does more than make it possible to fit your plant into a small container. Root-pruning stimulates growth, promotes health, and proportions the roots to the cut-back top. It is natural to be timid about cutting roots, but relax. Even severe root-pruning can be safe. In fact, more than half the roots can be cut away without danger. Later, on other plants, you can remove even more by root-pruning in stages.

Now, remove soil only from roots you plan to cut. I avoid the traditional Japanese method of doing this with chopsticks since prodding may cut and bruise roots. You can gently work the soil free with your hands or wash it off with water, as I do.

The root-ball can be cut with a knife, hatchet, or shears. Shears are safe and fast. First slice across the bottom, cutting parallel with the soil surface (unless your tree is to be planted *at an angle* to the pot; then make the bottom cut parallel to the container). Trim off uneven roots that remain. The base of the root-ball should be flat: this promotes the development of a shallow, spreading root system.

Your tree is now ready for potting. Select a conventional bonsai container with at least one drain hole in the bottom. Cover the hole with fine wire or nylon mesh, then add a layer of quarter-inch pea gravel or sponge-rock (perlite) for drainage. The drainage layer should be no thicker than one-fourth the depth of a shallow container, nor more than one inch in a deeper pot.

Cover the drainage material with a sprinkling of soil. Next position the tree, spreading its roots throughout the container. Hold the tree in place and put soil around the roots. Strike the container smartly as you work to settle the soil. Keep the soil about one-quarter inch below the top of the container—to prevent erosion. Pack it gently with your fingers.

Finally water your bonsai. If you can, moisten first by soaking in water slightly deeper than the container. If you cannot do this, sprinkle the tree gently from above. Ground-covers, moss for example, can be added if you wish.

You could now begin training your tree with wire, but your bonsai will respond better after a rest. Keep it in full shade for a week, then gradually increase the amount of sun until your new bonsai receives the full amount needed by the species. Properly cared for your instant bonsai will grow in stature and beauty as your knowledge of the art increases.

(*Above*), We begin with a Japanese black pine purchased locally for less than $2.00. The tree has been removed from its tin can but you could wait to remove the container until after you organize this tangle of branches. (*Below*), Preliminary pruning brings us to this point. I have trimmed basal branches, to open the trunk, and removed two branches near the center to eliminate cross-overs.

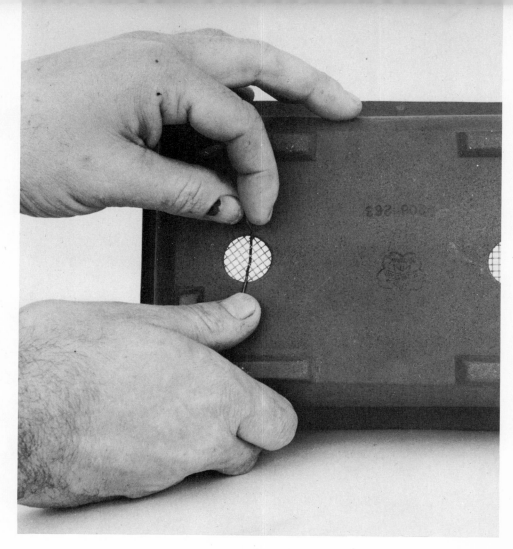

(*Above*), I block the drains with wire-screen. These are held in place with copper "staples." (*Below*), A drainage layer of quarter-inch pea gravel (or quarter-inch clay granules) is spread over the bottom. I also like an inert material such as perlite.

69

(*Above*), The root-ball is trimmed to fit the container and also to reduce the mass so that it is in proportion to the top. Base is cut parallel with the surface soil and dangling roots are cut away. (*Below*), Earth is scraped from the surface so that this slopes away from the trunk, giving the tree a better "landscaped" appearance.

(*Above*), The tree is positioned in the container with a concern for balance and visual weight. (*Below*), Potting soil is added and worked in around the roots.

The approach to pruning here is the same as in the Orient. With bonsai, it is a matter of degree and of proper timing. Most pruning is done at the end of the dormant season when sap is rising and plants are about to reach peak strength. Fast growers can be pruned earlier than slow ones. I shape the Japanese hornbeam (*Carpinus japonica*) before buds break their casings, but I rarely touch beech, especially the Japanese *Fagus sieboldii*, until buds have had time to elongate and leaves begin to open.

Years ago I discovered at least one exception to the early-pruning rule. Among my first bonsai was a lovely Japanese flowering cherry. I shaped the tree in spring and waited for an exciting display. Of course, few blossoms opened, and I learned with horror what most gardeners knew: flower buds lie dormant in leaf axils. I had cut them away. Now I do not prune flowering trees until *after they bloom.*

Pruning is an essential part of shaping, and shaping is usually accomplished not, as with your instant bonsai, but in stages—pruning, potting, then wiring. The process can take a year or longer. Cautious growers watch the reaction of an important tree and proceed accordingly.

Your purpose is always to shape your tree to an ideal but typical form, not to make an exact copy. Let a formal style feature perfectly balanced branches, a symmetrical shape, and well-tapered top. Let an informal style show an easy, exciting curve in the trunk. Try to style a deciduous tree sensitively—a zelkova with the spreading, impressive geometry of a broom, a Japanese maple in the traditional wineglass.

On most trees, small cuts heal without first aid. The ginkgo is an exception; on this delicate species, even small cuts need attention. Protect them with pruning compound as you should protect more serious cuts on other trees. You will find that sometimes unsightly pruning scars cannot be avoided. However, if you chisel sharp edges inward with a carving tool to make a slight hollow, a wound will heal faster and smoother and be less likely to result in a visible scar.

When a long root is too tough to cut away, it can be shaped to a container without breaking by cutting it part way through with a razor blade. Make two or more cuts, on the underside, of the root, just as a carpenter notches wood to make it pliable. Such a heavy cut root will eventually adapt its growth to the new contour.

Separate fine roots so you can get at the larger inside roots. Cut away about half of these. Make cuts at right angles to the woody roots—and be brave. When you prune large roots, you promote the growth of ciliary roots, the small hairlike ones that draw in nutrition. Watch for root areas darker than the rest, probable signs of dead or dying wood. Remove these with sharp clean cuts.

This live oak is pruned to clean the trunk and branches sufficiently to define the form. Barrie Coate.

This Colorado spruce, collected from the mountains, has grown in this rock for three years. The deadwood, *jin*, especially on conifers, should not be pruned until you are sure it has no value. It can be the vital aspect of an unusual design. Bob and Peggy Krohn.

The beauty of bonsai lies in a combination of form, scale, and content. In designing you will discover that an awareness of nature is almost more helpful than a knowledge of art. This pyracantha is a fine example. Barrie Coate.

4. How to Wire and Train Bonsai

After you have established the basic design of your tree by pruning, use wire to help develop good form and correct any branch defects. The technique is simple. Malleable yet strong wire is wrapped around part of the tree, then the wired part is bent, and growth is forced to follow. In time the new contour becomes permanent. Any part of a bonsai can be wire-trained except the shoots that are less than two inches long.

Some plants are easy to train, as Japanese white pine and pyracantha, which can be safely wired spring through fall. Evergreens are best wired in spring and summer. I train pine and juniper as early as February. Most deciduous trees, maple is one, can be wired in spring, but wires should be removed the same year just after leaves fall. Zelkova should be wired late, mid-June through mid-July.

More than a dozen species can be safely wired in winter, including arborvitae, azalea, camellia, cedar, cypress, false-cypress, fir, holly, ivy, privet, pyracantha, quince, spruce, and yew.

A few trees like cherry are difficult to wire at any time. Wood is brittle when dormant and during growth the bark softens. When you twist wire around it, you risk twisting bark. Careful growers wire cherry only in mid-May, removing wires meticulously a month later. Zelkova is also wired only for short periods, two or three months at most. When I wire a delicate species, I protect the soft bark with a wrap of raffia or plastic-covered wire; on trees like the cherry, I use paper-wrapped wire.

Try to avoid any re-training. Make your first shaping the right one. Plan styling in advance, bending branches gently in several directions to see where they look best. At the start, alteration in the direction of a single branch often makes an amazing difference.

You can develop an individual style for each tree without violating its natural form. As a rule, branches on conifers are wired down, those on deciduous trees are wired horizontally or even upward. Direction depends on the way a tree grows in nature, and also on your purpose. If you want to create an impression of age, prune a tree with soft edges, clip terminal growth, and wire branch tips downward. If you want a tree to seem young, leave the terminal growth and train tips upward.

Copper is the traditional training wire; galvanized iron, a recent development, is used only by commercial growers. Iron wire is stiff, difficult, even dangerous. It can rust, cause stains, and rot the wood. Copper is easier to use and does not stain, but government demands could make it scarce. You may be able to adapt copper from electrical wiring; when you can't, substitute aluminum wire.

Uncovered wire is the usual choice but wire covered with paper or plastic, is best for trees with delicate bark. Plastic-covered electrician's wire can be used as it is, but I strip off the plastic because it makes the wire bulky and too prominent. Admittedly, the choice is a matter of taste.

You need several gauges to adapt the wire to the thickness and stiffness of branches and trunk. If you want a complete supply, buy all gauges from No. 4 to No. 24; if you want only the essentials, order two or three gauges between No. 10 and No. 20, plus a length of No. 4 or No. 6 for thick wood. These last two are sold by hardware and electrical shops as "grounding wire." It comes unwrapped by the pound. Number 8 to No. 16 gauges are common electrical sizes, available in one- to five-wire cables; No. 10 to No. 20 gauges are also sold unwrapped, in 25- and 50-foot spools.

In Japan, copper wire is annealed, that is, heated over a straw fire to proper temperature and a dull red color, and then cooled. Annealing softens wire and dims the surface. Much of our electrically-treated wire needs only dulling. You can anneal and dull wire in the fireplace above burning newspapers or over the flame of a gas range. I use an all-purpose butane torch to work small quantities. Avoid overheating; it makes wire too brittle.

Annealed wires are practical for most trees, but for a few, uncovered wires absorbing the sun's rays, get too hot and cause bark-burn. Paper-covered wires avoid this danger.

If you are using several gauges of wire, arrange them in order on your worktable. This avoids confusion. When you wire, start at the base of a tree, first with the trunk, then go on to the lower limbs. As you work up, the branches below should be finished and ready for reference. Notes may help and I often make a rough sketch as a guide to the shape I want. Photographs with changes marked in grease pencil are also useful.

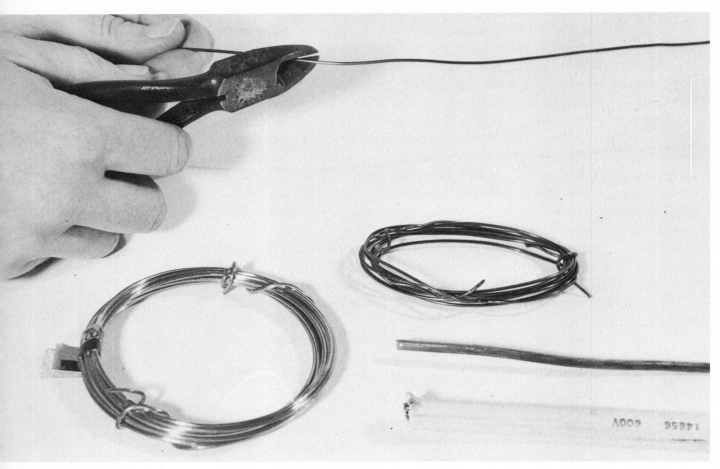

(*Above*), You need several gauges of wire; some types are sold unwrapped. (*Below*), Others can be adapted from plastic-wrapped electrical wiring; heavy gauges come with several strands.

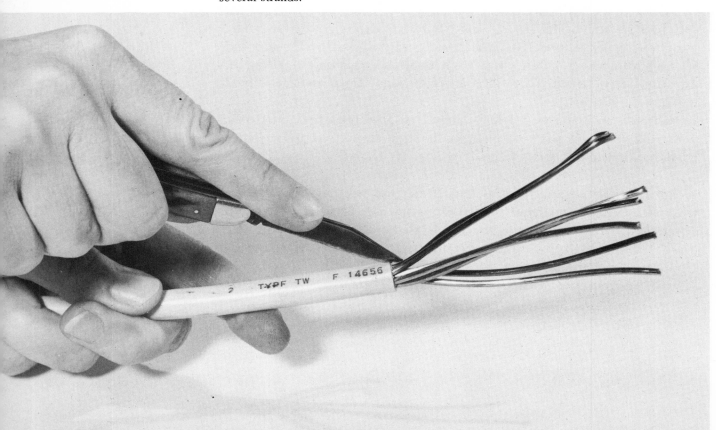

Most trees require three gauges of wire. A good working rule is this: use thinner wire when a tree is growing, thicker wire when it is dormant. The *right* wire is the thinnest that will hold a branch. Thick wire is unsightly, difficult to use, and when it must be removed, harmful. If your heaviest wire is not strong enough, use two strands. Wrap the second wire parallel to the first.

Wrap the wire in spirals, on one-inch centers. But spacing is not critical so long as the individual wrappings are neither too far apart (with little holding power) nor too close (with a serious chance of scarring). Within reason, the individual wraps can be moved closer or farther apart to alter holding power. When maximum power is needed, use the wire close together.

Don't wire buds and leaves. You can avoid them easily on most trees, but on pines it may be difficult. One end of the wire must always be firmly anchored. When you work on the trunk, anchor the wire by inserting one end in the ground and as close to the tree as possible. When you wire a branch or the top of a tree, anchor the wire to another limb or to the trunk. You can work from the spool or with lengths of wire. I find it easier, and safer, to work with short precut pieces.

In practice the wire is wrapped around the area you plan to shape while the tree is at rest. After the wire is fixed, bend the branch to its new direction. This bending is as close to sculpturing as any phase of bonsai. You form new shapes by feel. Work slowly with both hands to avoid breaking or twisting a limb. Although wire can be wound in right- or left-hand spirals, it is better to wrap in the direction you will bend the branch. In this way the wire tightens rather than loosens. When growth is particularly stiff and difficult to bend, it may help to preshape it two or three times. "Working a branch" often makes it supple. In any case, bend the wood slowly.

To make shaping easier, I fertilize bonsai a month or so before wiring. Feeding promotes the flow of sap, tones the tree, makes it sturdier, and so reduces the danger of shock. The result is that limbs are more pliable to work.

Stiff, woody branches can be handled with greater safety if you reduce the water supply. I often decrease water-intake progressively two or three days in advance. With deciduous species, such as ginkgo and maple, I stop watering six to eight hours before wiring.

If my styling notes call for abrupt changes in contour, I may do the work in stages. In rare cases, when nothing else works, I make a small cut on the underside of the wood at the apex of the bend. This reduces strain and minimizes chances of breakage. If you try this, make a shallow, V-shaped cut as small as possible. Small cuts heal quickly and may not leave scars. Large ones can split limbs.

When wiring is finished, set the tree in a shady place for a week or two. Water frequently, misting leaves the first two days. *A tree that is weak or has recently been repotted should not be wired; a tree that has been recently wired should not be repotted.*

Be sure to remove wires before they can disfigure bark. Timing depends on growth rate. As a tree grows, bark can be forced between and around wire. Eventually, pressure restricts the flow of sap. Scars can develop fast. Permanent injury may result.

Keep in mind that a tree goes on growing. Wires that are loose today may be tight in a month or two. Check them frequently. While wire marks are commonly avoided for aesthetic reasons, some collectors use them creatively, claiming that, "A few marks, in selected areas, can age a young bonsai, giving it character."

OTHER TRAINING METHODS

Wiring is not a panacea, but when it is used along with pinching, it assures certain results. Yet not all growers favor wiring and not all in favor have equal enthusiasm for it. Many claim wires are "unnatural," and prefer to depend upon weights, ropes, and guy lines.

Branches *can* be weighted to new shapes, a technique favored a century ago in Japan. In the Meiji period, growers condemned wires and used rock-weights. Lead fishing sinkers now do a good job. Available in various weights, they can be scaled to the job. The sinkers can be tied to branches with string, but I prefer monofilament fishing line because it is almost invisible; some prefer to attach wires to the weights. Whatever you use, anchor weights to keep them from shifting.

New shapes can be developed by *tying* branches to the trunk, to other branches, and to the container. Ropes, wires, and guy lines help to create the flowing curves that make good cascades. Be sure to protect bark with a piece of thick plastic or a section of rubber inner tube. There are various ways to improvise a "natural" approach. One enthusiast places wire screen over low-growing alpines. "It's like the natural weight of snow," she claims.

What is your best approach? Wires? Ropes and guy lines? Weights? Consider them all. If wiring seems questionable and you are one of the rare growers who can be satisfied with a completely "natural" bonsai trained to less than a predictable form, then forget wiring. If you like to control the growing process as far as possible, include wiring in your bag of tricks. But use wire with the delicacy it demands, and your bonsai will be the more attractive for it.

3. Four flowering fruit trees make charming bonsai; two of quince on the left, two of apricot on the right. Y. Sato.

4. Maples are favorites with bonsai-growers the world over, especially the Japanese and the trident. John Dutro.

(*Above*), Wrap wire in spirals with one end firmly anchored; for trunk-wiring, anchor in the ground beside the tree. (*Below*), The closeness of the centers depends on the tension required; one-inch centers are usual. Closer centers have greater holding power.

(*Above*), An example of how not to wire; spirals are loose, wrapping uneven. (*Below*), Wire marks are more likely when two wires overlap. Use technique with caution.

(*Above*), On soft-barked trees or in areas where gentle training is required, use loose wiring. (*Below*), When the heaviest wire will not hold, use two or three strands. Shape the wire to the branch, then secure with other wires at right angles to the trunk. Both, Yoshio Sato.

83

Wires do not have to be wrapped to be effective, as on this Japanese apricot tree, called *ume* or *mume*. With ends tied to the branch and the trunk, enough pressure can be exerted to train gentle curves with less risk. Yoshio Sato.

Weights also do a good job of training; or tie wires from branches to container as with this dwarf Alberta spruce. Remo Zaro.

On this Atlantic blue cedar, wiring is combined with another support, a rock. Wire marks, shown near the top, are usually avoided, although some growers feel that they foster an impression of age. Yoshio Sato.

Branches can be tied safely with raffia, as on this *Juniperus procumbens,* and a tie-down is less likely to mark a tree. Gaye Donaldson.

87

5.   Potting Soils and Fertilizers

Potting soils are custom-made. Some growers insist on a formula for each species; some require different soils for different stages of development; others use three or more kinds of soils, in layers, for each potting. But most of us favor a simpler approach. We discover that beautiful bonsai can be grown with just a few mixtures, perhaps only three: one for conifers, one for deciduous plants and other evergreens, and a third for flowering and fruiting varieties.

SOIL BASICS Soils that make up any potting mixture are a complex of mineral and organic or humus particles. The minerals have weathered and eroded from rocks whose type affects the acidity and alkalinity of the soil. Igneous rocks, those created by heat, as granite and gneiss, usually form acid soils. Sediment rocks, as shale and limestone, form more neutral soils. Organic particles come from decayed matter—plant, bacterial, and animal. Organic or humus elements help to separate the mineral particles and have an affect upon both nutrition and soil chemistry. All soils are a mixture of the two materials.

The size of particles is a measure of soil texture. At one end of the scale is sand, the largest; at the other end, clay, the smallest. Sand has a few specialized uses, but it is correct to say that alone, neither sand nor clay will do for bonsai. Sand is porous and retains neither moisture nor nutrients. Clay packs tight, becomes waterlogged, and, by itself, is the least suitable of all possibilities. Natural soils contain varying ratios of sand and clay.

Plants require some sixteen elements or nutrients, the amount of each already in soil depends on local factors. Soils from areas that have long been cultivated and have little natural humus left and those that get enough rain to leach nutrients deep may lack some essentials. However, natural foods are not a primary concern. Many bonsai-growers consider their lack an asset. Missing nutrients can be added in *controlled* quantities.

Potting Soils

Potting mixtures are formulated in an attempt to produce ideal soil for bonsai. Basic elements include loam—a *natural* mixture of sand and clay—pure sand, and humus. The most common mixture is made from equal parts of loam and sand; variations sometimes include clay soils and humus.

Loam comes from the top layer or top two layers of soil, which varies in depth from two inches to more than two feet. The layer below the top is called subsoil; generally it is harder and of a different color. Below subsoil is a tough, clay strata called hardpan. Hardpan has no value for bonsai.

Potting mixes can be made with top soil or with subsoil. Sometimes a combination is used. The top soil is usually rich in humus and nutrition. Subsoils are generally cleaner—free of contamination from insects, bacteria, and virus.

Use both soils. If contamination becomes a problem, soils can be disinfected. (Sterilization, the common term, implies the death of all organisms, beneficial as well as harmful, and that is not what you want.) Small quantities of soil can be sufficiently purified with boiling water. This will control nematodes and fungi but six gallons of water are required per cubic foot of soil and, on the basis of quantity alone, the technique is tiresome. Chemicals are only a little better. If formaldehyde is used, soil cannot be potted until the distinctive odor disappears. Heat is the easy answer. Put your soil in a shallow pan and bake it in a low oven for forty-five minutes; or you can buy sterilized soil. Actually only loam needs disinfecting. Sand, peat, and such inert additives as perlite and vermiculite are safe.

Is disinfecting worth the effort? I depend on it for first-time potting because it seems to give my plants an edge, but the antiseptic effect is quickly lost. Add a ground-cover at the last minute, and you may also add disease. Dirty tools can do the same. The use of disinfected soil must be accompanied by a sterile approach to potting.

Sand has sharp, definite granules that promote the growth of fine roots and also break up clay. If you live in a city, concrete-mix sand is a good choice. It is pure and available. Avoid seashore sand because of the salt content. If you can collect sand, do so. River sand is the very best. Mine comes from mountain streams near my home and is ideal. Much of it is weathered granite, with substantial quantities of iron—the perfect medium for conifers. Iron-sand promotes the growth of healthy green needles.

89

(*Above*), The drainage layer includes ¼-inch gravel, clay granules, or inert material. Sand is added to clay-loam soils; fine sands do not need screening. (*Below*), Many growers use ready-made Japanese screens, others build their own. A set of four will do, ¼-inch mesh for the largest screen, ⅟₃₂-inch for the smallest.

(*Above*), The potting layer can be made of a mixture from two screens, with an even finer top-dressing added for looks. (*Below*), Water intake is governed by drainage, and drainage is controlled by a layer of coarse gravel (*left*) or inert material (*right*).

Humus is added to some mixtures in various percentages, its purpose, to retain moisture and improve texture. Peat, leafmold, and compost are good humus additives, but avoid organic fertilizers. Organics supply nitrogen but do little for texture. Peat is available and easy to handle, although some types are acid. You can buy leafmold, and you can make your own. Some growers swear by broad-leaf deciduous mixtures, others want nothing but oak-leaf. Since I use very little humus, I confess I can scarcely tell the difference. I do avoid fine-leaf composts because they decompose into material that clogs drainage.

ACIDITY AND ALKALINITY

The symbol pH is used to indicate neutral, acid, and alkaline soil conditions; pH 7.0 is neutral. Lower numbers indicate acidity; higher, alkalinity. An extreme, in either direction, can affect the metabolism of a plant.

Alkalinity is common in areas with little rain; it is rarely harmful and usually can be controlled by watering. Many "hard" waters—those containing magnesium and calcium qualify—help leach away alkaline salts. Softened water is hardly beneficial. Water softeners produce chemical changes in water than can be more harmful to plants than the condition they supposedly correct.

Acidity is common in wet soils—usually in regions with more than thirty inches of rain—but there are exceptions along the Coast. Native plants are guides to acidity. If acid-loving azaleas, blueberries, or laurel grow where you collect potting loam, you need no other yardstick. If a more neutral soil is not available, it may be easier to buy neutral packaged soils than to try to reduce acidity with chemicals.

SCREENING

A good potting mixture has three objectives: easy rooting, fast drainage, and good nutrition. Texture, the key to rooting and drainage, is achieved by sizing soil particles through screens. Sand does not need to be screened.

Many growers use Japanese screens, available here from specialists. Kits include seven graduated screens with from three to thirty or more wires per inch. The seven come in a nest, and are used with one on top of another. Soils passing through the screens are thus separated into seven textures of varying coarseness, and the seven soils are then separately stored and labeled. I build my own screens, and currently use four: ¼-inch is the biggest mesh: 1⁄32-inch is the smallest. Frames are made of 1-by-2 lumber, and the largest is 12-by-12 inches.

Corners can be mitered or butt-jointed depending more on the amount of carpentry involved than on the subsequent strength of the frames. So long as corners are glued or reinforced with metal plates it doesn't matter. Spread out the piece of screening on a flat surface; then bend up the edges to form sides about ½ inch high. Secure with staples, lath, or with both.

Dry out soil to be screened for a week or longer before you work it. Crush the lumps and work smaller particles through the mesh with a circular motion.

The sizes of soil particles you save will depend on your potting method. Coarse material that will not pass through the ¼-inch screen should be thrown away. Quarter-inch material is right for the bottom drainage layer. Save it if you prefer to use such natural clay granules. Some growers like ¼-inch gravel; others use an inert material like perlite. I prefer perlite for most jobs.

Soils caught by the two finer screens, $\frac{1}{16}$-inch and $\frac{1}{32}$-inch are stored separately. Later they are combined as my standard potting mix. The finer material, which works through all four screens, is collected and spread on my compost pile.

Some twelve years ago scientists at the University of California developed a new medium for container plants, the basis a disease-free compound called the U.C. Mix. Although it has not yet been widely used for bonsai, it has exciting possibilities for experiment. It is a combination of sand, peatmoss (redwood sawdust or bark is sometimes substituted), and fertilizers. The texture promotes the development of fine roots, and as a rule, fine roots produce smaller leaves.

The U.C. Mix has many good effects: aeration, easy watering, good leaching, for example. The medium cannot become waterlogged and would be well worth trying if you live in a damp area.

I am testing it on four azaleas planted three years ago; so far results are promising. If there is a drawback to the formula, it may be that when bark or sawdust is substituted for peat, the Mix becomes slightly acid. For more information about it, write to the Agricultural Extension Service of the University of California, at Berkeley.

Fertilizers

What makes a plant grow? Nearly three hundred years ago a Flemish scientist, Jan van Helmont, sought the answer. He planted a willow in a measured container of dry soil, watered the tree over a period of five years, then removed it. After drying the soil, he weighed it again. The soil had lost two ounces, yet the willow had gained 165 pounds. Van Helmont decided that "Water made the tree grow."

This myth persists, but scientists now know that the truth lies in the missing two ounces of soil and also in the air. The lost ounces accounted for elements drawn from the soil; these, combined with carbon and oxygen from the air and hydrogen from water, made the tree grow.

As we have said, sixteen chemicals, scientists call them elements, are necessary for plant growth. Six are needed in relatively large, ten in small amounts. Let's examine the most important elements.

Nitrogen This promotes growth. It comes from the air and from micro-organisms and electrical action in soil. Easily lost through leaching, it does not occur in all soils. It is included in most fertilizers. We avoid heavy use of nitrogen in spring because it is likely to cause runaway growth.

Phosphorus Used as phosphate iron, this promotes root development and the formation of flower buds. Most soils contain adequate amounts. Those that are neutral or slightly acid usually have more than alkaline soils do.

Potassium Called potash, this also helps to promote root growth and to maintain a balance between nitrogen and phosphorus. Potash appears to retard the rapid growth that excess nitrogen may generate, and also helps plants to endure low temperatures and ward off disease. It may have an effect on the size and color of fruit. Many soils are lacking in potash.

Calcium Called lime, this works as a catalyst with phosphorus and potassium, making them readily available to plants. Essential for some plants, lime can be detrimental to ericaceous or acid-loving plants, such as azaleas. Small amounts can be used to lighten clay soils.

Trace elements A host of lesser chemicals—iron, manganese, copper, zinc, molybdenum, and boron—plus twenty-two more are considered beneficial but not essential. Iron is the most important of these, a catalyst in the production of chlorophyll, and essential to photosynthesis, the manufacture of sugars and starches within the leaves.

RAPESEED AND
OTHER FERTILIZERS

Japanese growers rely on natural vegetable and animal compounds to supply nutrition. Vegetable fertilizers, including rapeseed (*Brassica napus*), cottonseed, and soybean, are made up in cakes and powders. Animal fertilizers include bonemeal, fishmeal, whole dried fish, and, in limited amount, chicken manure.

A common fertilizer is made from rapeseed cakes or powder dissolved in water. While rapeseed is not readily available here, some importers handle it. I obtain mine by mail and prefer it to most fertilizers because it contains nitrogen, phosphorus, and potassium, in a 5-3-2 ratio, which many of us consider an ideal ratio for bonsai.

If you use rapeseed fertilizer, make it yearly, as early as February if possible. Mix the cake or powder with water, then let the brew ferment through mid-March or early April. I like this formula:

> One part rapeseed cake or powder to 10 to 12 parts water. Stir well, cover, and store in a cool, dry place. Dilute 15 to 35 times and use two to three tablespoons per tree per application. I add a pinch of bonemeal for each flowering and fruiting tree, and a tablespoonful of wood ashes per quart of mix when soils need conditioning.

Try rapeseed pellets, easily made with rapeseed and water alone, or with rapeseed, water, and fishmeal, bonemeal, or wood ashes, and an equal amount of potting loam. Form into half-inch balls. Insert the pellets or balls in the soil, an easy way to fertilize rock plantings; use one or two for each.

I also use dried fish when I repot. The finger-sized fish, are available from stores in Japanese-American communities but I've never seen them elsewhere. I put two or three fish in each pot.

Most American growers rely on commercial fertilizers, and I do too. Labels indicate the ratio of the three principal ingredients, nitrogen, phosphorus, and potassium. A 7-7-15, for example, contains 7 percent nitrogen, 7 percent phosphoric acid, and 15 percent potash. Regardless of ratio, the three chemicals are always shown in this order.

I use liquids and powders as well. High-analysis fertilizers, in which the three figures total more than thirty, are more expensive, and in my opinion, hardly necessary for bonsai. The standard mixtures whose figures total less than thirty are safer. I particularly like Hyponex in liquid or powder form, the 7-6-19 ratio seems excellent for bonsai. I use about four grams (one teaspoon) to a gallon of water; the powder dissolves quickly and can be used at once.

Another liquid I like is called 0-10-10; it is made by several manufacturers, sometimes with vegetable extract added. This is excellent for early spring because it has no nitrogen, and especially good for flowering plants.

YEAR-ROUND SCHEDULE

Whatever fertilizer you use, apply it on a regular schedule, and keep in mind that overfertilizing at any time can generate soft unsightly growth. Here is my schedule:

Spring Monthly applications for deciduous trees and conifers. Twice monthly for other evergreens and young trees; extra helping for mature bonsai in May. I don't fertilize during rainy periods, and I stop the fertilizing of fruiting and flowering trees as soon as they start to bloom.

Summer Monthly applications for most trees but none for flowering and fruiting species until fruit is set; twice monthly for conifers and once a month for other evergreens. The strength of the applications is gradually increased through this season but I don't fertilize at all during periods of excessive heat.

Fall The schedule tapers off now, as does the strength of applications. Deciduous trees are fertilized after leaves fall, but not later than the end of October; evergreens through October. Flowering and fruiting trees get an application of liquid fertilizer. Fall fertilizing helps thicken trunks of young trees.

Winter No fertilizing.

Loam is an indefinite term; if the loam in your area contains a high percentage of sand, cut it with clay subsoils; if it seems clayey, cut it with sand.

Mixture	Loam	Sand	Humus	Notes
Bottom mix	1 part ¼-inch clay granules	1 part ¼-inch pea gravel	None	Inert materials like perlite can be used alone, but if you prefer a natural base, this mix is good.
Top mix	Standard loam or	2 parts	None	A good standard mix. Screen loams through $\frac{1}{16}$- and $\frac{1}{32}$-inch screens.
	1 part clay, 1 part clay subsoil	2 parts	1 part	
Seed mix	1 part	1 part	None	Excellent for most seedlings.

Conifer

Conifer mix	½	½	None	
Alternate conifer mix	⅓	⅔		Best for trees, such as pines, that require dry soil.

Deciduous Trees and Evergreens

Deciduous mix	½	¼	¼	For acid-loving plants, such as azaleas, reduce loam slightly and increase humus.
Alternate deciduous mix	¾	¾	None	Popular in Japan, but plants require more fertilization.

| Mix | ½ | ⅜ | ⅛ |

The mixtures above are generally adequate, but if you want to experiment with specific mixtures, these are suggested:

| Ginkgo | ½ fine
¼ standard | ⅛ | ⅛ |
| Zelkova | ¾ | ¼ | |

6. *The Art of Potting and Repotting*

Potting, simply defined as "planting in a container" is a one-time, first-time activity. A subsequent change in pots is termed repotting. You can plant your freshly-pruned trees in shallow, traditional bonsai containers or in deeper training pots that will hold more roots and so involve less root-pruning at the start. Potting procedures are the same. Let your choice of container be guided by the welfare of each plant rather than by your desire for a quick effect.

To Pot a Plant   If you decide to plant directly in a bonsai container choose one in which the tree looks "right" or because tradition indicates such a shape, size, or color. Select a training pot for a realistic reason—space. Use new pots without cleaning, but scrupulously clean used ones. Remove all traces of soil, and if there is danger of infection from a previous unhealthy tenant, scrub with hot soapy water to which a touch of household bleach has been added. Do a thorough job; rinse two or three times, then invert to drain. Let containers dry until the smell of bleach is no longer noticeable.

IMPORTANCE OF DRAINAGE   I'd be a wealthy man if I had a dime for every time someone said to me, "Water is the secret of bonsai." The cliché implies it is impossible to overwater and, of course, that is nonsense. Too much water is dangerous. It makes soil sour, airless, and waterlogged, a crippling, killing condition.

One bonsai "doctor," a nurseryman who handles hundreds of sick trees every year, told me root damage, triggered by improper drainage, accounts for seven tenths of the failures he treats. "The sad part is the problem could be avoided," he lamented, "Bonsai containers and training pots have good drain holes."

98

Some growers prefer to soak new unglazed pots half an hour or so before potting on the theory that presoaking makes first watering easier and more reliable. I soak newly-potted plants *after* potting as a matter of course and get much the same result. Instead of presoaking, I begin by partially blocking the drains to keep in the soil as the water seeps out. Broken crockery laid loosely over the holes will work but I prefer squares of quarter-inch mesh—called hardware cloth in some areas. By any name quarter-inch mesh is neater, safer, and more efficient. Be sure the squares are at least an inch larger than the drains.

You can secure screen by depressing the center into the drainage hole with a blunt stick or your thumb. Or you can fashion U-shaped staples from copper wire. Push the "legs" through from the inside; then bend them outward on the bottom.

The water-intake of bonsai is limited by the potting mix, or more accurately, in part by a layer of coarse drainage material over the bottom of the container. The material lets water through quickly, and the soil retains only the amount a plant can use. Usually the drainage mix is quarter-inch pea gravel or clay granules of about the same size. I use both but my favorite is perlite or sponge-rock, a volcanic derivative that promotes quick drainage yet retains some moisture. It reduces the work of watering. Eastern growers have recently experimented with two new baked-clay products: Terra-Green (Oil Dri Corporation) and Turface (Wyandotte Chemical Corporation). Reports indicate good results.

Whatever drainage material you use, spread it over the bottom of the container to about one fifth the depth. If you like to add solid fertilizer, dried fish for example, put it here, then place the layer of potting soil. Spread this layer thinly, leaving space for the tree roots.

A rock and clump of mondo grass or lily-turf (*Ophiopogon*) set off this spruce, *Picea glauca conica.* Gaye Donaldson.

POSITIONING A TREE

When you pot in a training container, center a tree so new roots will grow in all directions. When you plant in a bonsai container, position a tree for maximum visual interest. A tree always looks best in just one particular place in each container.

Your objective is to create an effect of nature in miniature, so placement is important. Bonsai are often centered in round and square containers but planted off-center in oval and rectangular ones. Formal upright trees are almost always centered, as are double-trunk trees and small group plantings.

In bonsai culture, "centered" is a visual not a mathematical term. It means to the *rear* of the measured center, and a tree usually seems in better balance when it is a little inclined toward the front. In off-center plantings, Japanese artists usually rely on the rule of thirds. The trunk is planted at a point that is equal to two-thirds the longer dimension of the container.

A moss ground-cover for this grove of Japanese five-needle pine contributes to the design. Dan Buckley.

You can often do a more artistic—and less mechanical—job when you imagine the container as a stretch of open land. The tree then has "weight," a visual concept you can translate as balance and imbalance. For example, when a tree is heavy with branches on the right it looks best, or balances better, planted closer to the left side of the container.

The same principle is at work with front branches. They can make a tree appear unstable and unbalanced. If they can't be removed, possibly you can reverse the position of the trunk. At the back, these same branches may add to the illusion of depth.

Once the tree is positioned, spread the roots fanlike around the pot to stabilize the trunk and help the plant absorb a full quota of moisture. Then add soil.

If you haven't heard the controversy over soil density, you will. Some growers insist soil should be tightly packed; others that it be reasonably loose. You will have to take sides because density does influence the amount of moisture a soil-mix retains. A loose mix has plenty of holes and spaces. It may drain quickly, but these spaces retain a fair amount of moisture. A hard-packed soil works the opposite way, retaining little moisture. Since I believe most plants need a moderately moist environment, I'm on the side of the loose-soilers.

Ferns enhance this rock-grown maple. Trees and rock should not be separated when they are repotted. John A. Dutro.

One day I watched Yoshio Sato, a famous California grower, potting. He poured soil over freshly-pruned roots, leveling it just below the container lip to prevent erosion. Then he struck the pot sharply with the heel of his hand to settle the soil around the roots. He gently packed it from the top with his fingers. "If the soil needed to be tighter, I would use a mallet," he explained, "but loose soil is better except for pines. Give them hard-packed soil. They need less water. Some growers pack soil around roots with chopsticks. The theory is that sticks force soil into spaces you otherwise miss. Avoid sticks even when they make you feel like a bonsai-master. They can damage delicate roots."

HOLD-DOWNS New bonsai can often stand proud and sure without aid, but when a tree seems shaky, don't take chances. Count on six months for new roots to grow. The more stable a tree is during that period the longer and stronger the new roots will become.

There are various ways to stabilize trees. Some growers use wet soil, pressing mounds of mud around the roots as they pot. The trick works although the hard-packed earth reduces the number of water-holding air pockets. I prefer the simple method of placing a rock, as if it were a paperweight, over the soil-covered surface roots. Sometimes one or two rocks are needed beside the trunk for extra support. The rocks rarely contribute to the effect, but they are a natural approach and therefore desirable. I remove them in six months.

In difficult cases, I tie the tree; this procedure depends on the shape of the pot. When I can, I simply wrap a string around the trunk and under the pot. When a pot has a lip, I tie one string horizontally below it, and use this string as tie-point for others. Sometimes two or three strings can be arranged like guy wires; sometimes the only solution is to use tie-downs inside the pot. The arrangement depends on the number of drains in the container.

Single-drain hold-downs Use a length of wire or string long enough to reach twice the distance from the base of the container to a point two inches above soil level. Wrap the center of it around a stick or button larger than the drain and force the free ends through the drain. These can be wrapped around the trunk above the soil or around the roots below soil-level.

(*Above*), Ferns and grasses, especially the mondos (*far right*) can be used as ground-covers or accents. Select for scale as well as color. (*Below*), Consider baby's-tears, a tender fast-growing ground-cover that may prove temporary. Since it likes water, use with trees that need moisture.

(*Above left*), Fill a container with potting mix, then spread cheesecloth to make it easier to handle moss. (*Right*), Sprinkle moss over cheesecloth, mixing with sand if difficult. (*Below left*), Cover with a second layer of cheesecloth, and water; put in cool shaded place. (*Right*), In ninety days, cut thick verdant moss into pieces with knife or scissors.

(*Above left*), Cut the root-ball with trowel, shears, or hatchet. (*Right*), Slope the surface for effect. (*Below*), Prune away some branches.

(*Above*), The pruned juniper is placed over the drainage layer. (*Below*), Using rocks as hold-downs, keep tree in position until roots develop.

Two-drain hold-downs Use two lengths of string or wire. Tie one end of each around a stick or button; force the free end through the drain and pull. The free ends can be joined or tied around the roots individually. Tie-downs work well if they do not girdle trunk or roots.

Some growers use wire as a matter of course. I don't. I prefer string because it does not scar. The new nylon strings are strong, yet they rot in a few months, eliminating the problem of girdling.

After the tree has been tied down and potted, it should be watered. Make the first watering a gentle one, either a soft top-spray or a soaking. I'm a dues-carrying member of the soaking brigade. Soaking does not dislodge soil and is sure, thorough, and safe. Here is my method:

Place the pot in water at least half as deep as the container. Leave it until the surface soil *feels* damp. Remove the pot, drain carefully, and mist the foliage to reduce the shock of transplanting.

Some growers prefer a full soaking, and I can agree with them. Horace Hinds, an experienced amateur from the San Francisco Bay Area, gave this good description of soaking in *Bonsai*, the excellent magazine he and his wife publish for Bonsai Clubs International:

"Submerge the pot in water until all bubbles are gone—about five minutes. Remove and drain. Place the tree in a protected spot for one week (if it is early in the year), or three weeks (later in the season)."

You can start wiring once a bonsai is potted, but if you have the patience to wait three to six months, the tree will benefit. Instead of accelerating the bonsai-process give the tree care. Water it daily, and after the luxury of one to three weeks in the shade, adjust it slowly to its full quota of sun.

To Repot a Plant

Bonsai need repotting, that is new soil and root-pruning, intermittently. Some require a shift once a year, some twice a decade. Obviously, there is danger of neglect in a schedule that must be so indefinite.

Agronomists at the University of Iowa proved the importance of prompt repotting when they raised an experimental rye plant in a cubic foot of soil—about three times the amount allotted to most bonsai. The rye was removed after four months and its underground growth measured. The finding: 385 miles of roots.

Fortunately, bonsai do not grow with the speed of rye. However, trees can develop surprising root systems in a short time, and it is claimed a plant is not growing well unless it becomes root-bound in two to three years.

Crowding is only one source of trouble. Oxygen depletion is another. Soil must contain an adequate supply of oxygen before roots can absorb moisture. Crowding diminishes the reserve. Soil must be light enough to let fine roots penetrate. Lack of aeration makes soil heavy, hard, and waterlogged, conditions that kill root ends. Then a tree develops slowly and erratically; foliage appears listless and unhealthy. But remove the tree from its pot, prune roots by as little as one-fourth, and provide new soil: you replace oxygen, you add nutrition, you eliminate problems.

Start repotting early in warm regions. Growers in southern California and Texas, for example, begin as early as February. I live in the mountains, at a higher altitude, 3000 feet, and consequently wait until April. But whatever month marks the beginning, repot while the sap flows fresh. Plants have their greatest strength then.

Commence with your early-flowering trees. Repot them before buds develop. Then attend to evergreen and deciduous varieties. Finish early. As a rule, fall repotting is dangerous: it leaves little time for trees to become established before winter. But there are exceptions.

Evergreens missed in spring can be repotted in fall when they have a second growth. Azaleas can be repotted into September; they are sturdy with shallow, compact roots. Ezo spruce and some nut-bearing species thrive on September and October pottings. Winter-flowering varieties are repotted after blooming but before they develop shoots. Bonsai raised under glass or indoors can be repotted any time, and when repotting consists only of switching containers, even outdoor bonsai can be handled safely in any season.

Timing depends more on the condition of the plant, its roots and soil, than on any manmade timetable. As long as there is an inch of open soil between roots and container, a plant does not need repotting. Young trees will probably need new soil yearly. A few species that grow rapidly, such as crape-myrtle and willow, may need attention twice a year. You'll repot young deciduous trees every two to three years and older ones every five to six. Check flowering and fruiting species twice a year. Young conifers can go three to four years; older ones may go twice as long.

Mame can be repotted on similar schedules, but many growers repot sooner because the small amount of soil contains so little oxygen and nutrition. One San Francisco grower, Mrs. Helena Renick, does not fertilize her *mame*. Instead she repots yearly. Most *mame* are repotted in spring but fruiting varieties in fall.

Schedule repotting in advance by going over your plants twice a year, spring and fall. As you check, be alert for the three emergency situations that call for immediate repotting:

1 *Pests* If worms, ants, or other insects cannot be controlled by sprays, repot without delay in fresh, clean soil. Sterilize the container, but not the soil.

2 *Soil* If the potting mix becomes hard-packed or waterlogged, replace it as soon as possible. Good drainage is the most important single requirement of bonsai.

(*Above left*), This smoke tree has just been transplanted from a training pot where it developed early form. (*Right*), Centered is a visual term, not a mathematical one. This hawthorn, *Crataegus oxyacantha,* is in the rear of the actual center and inclined forward. (*Below left*), To be sure of proper aeration and drainage, this *Euonymous alata* has been planted in loose soil. Gaye Donaldson. (*Right*), Rather than heavy root-pruning, which might weaken it, this Colorado spruce has been put in a larger training pot. Mrs. Emil Steinegger.

3 *Roots* If roots are damaged by overfertilization or by too much or too little water, repot immediately.

When a tree will not lift easily from the container, try pushing a stick through the drainage holes. Stubborn plants can also be freed by inverting the container and tapping gently. Or run a knife around the inside edge, then invert the plant.

After the container is removed, place the tree on a clean working surface, remove the large-granule drainage mixture from the bottom, then soil from the sides of the root-ball. Before repotting, keep your tree dry for twenty-four hours; the work goes easier in dry soil than in wet.

The amount of soil to be removed depends upon the condition of the plant, its age, and the size of the root-ball. Take away enough to allow one to two inches of the fresh mixture to be packed between roots and container, but adjust the quantity to the tree. Remove less soil from evergreens, slightly more from deciduous trees. Evergreens produce too much new growth with large amount of fresh soil. Trees that demand a lot of nutrition, as fruiting and flowering varieties, do better with more soil.

ROOT TRIMMING

After you have cleared the root system, trim the exposed roots. Cut each straight across, rather than on a slant, to minimize the danger of rot. Cut the main lateral roots, thin the soil at the edges of the mass, and fan out the root system. If the root-ball seems too dense, remove alternate sections to increase the area for growth. Look for dark roots, usually a sign of deadwood. Trim roots that appear injured, also any that are overly vigorous.

If you plan to transplant to a smaller pot, do it now; if you plan to use the same container, clean it thoroughly. If there has been a chance of contamination, sterilize it.

Repotting follows the same procedure as potting. First cover drains to prevent loss of soil, then spread a layer of drainage mixture over the bottom of the container. Use quarter-inch pea gravel, screened clay subsoil granules, or perlite. If you prefer dried fish as a base fertilizer, add it now. Next spread your favorite potting mixture, then place the tree, *remembering it must not be planted deeper than it stood originally.* Rather, consider the possibility of a slightly higher position to expose surface roots. Fill in with soil, mounding it in from the edge of the container.

Do not pack the soil. This reduces ability to absorb water, minimizes growth of the hairlike roots, and increases leaf size. Keep surface soil about a quarter-inch below the rim of the container to receive water and prevent erosion.

Bonsai grown *in* or *on rocks* are never repotted. Instead, remove the ground-cover, wash away a quarter of the old soil, and replace it with new. Check young rock-grown spruces often. In the beginning, Ezo, for example, may develop very fast.

Trees grown *over rocks* should not be separated from the rocks but they can be separated from the soil in the bottom of the container. Prune roots in the free soil normally, then replace rock and tree as a unit in fresh soil.

Trees that have been recently wired should not be repotted.

How to Grow Ground-Covers

Take time to add ground-covers for color and contrast, to retain moisture, or to relieve the too-new look of a recently-potted plant. Few nurseries sell moss but most handle moss substitutes, such as *Selaginella* and baby's-tears, *Helxine*. As long as you select material in scale with a tree, you can use a variety of ground-covers.

True mosses have a texture and color that make them my first choice. Since I live where native mosses are plentiful, I collect my own. Chances are you can do the same. Almost every section of the country has varieties that can be found year-round.

In the country, look for moss on rocks, trees, and moist ground. In the city, you'll find it on shingles, in your garden, even on the edge of a walk. Moss is wonderfully hardy. Pieces that have been dried for months can be revived with water. Collect a handful and you can grow your own. All you need is a shallow box and some soil.

To grow moss, put an inch or more of potting mix in a wooden flat or small container. A drainage layer is not essential. I spread a layer of cheesecloth because it makes the moss easier to handle, but cheesecloth is not essential. Dry the moss in a cool place until it can be crumbled, then sprinkle it over soil or the cheesecloth. If you have trouble handling the moss, mix it with sand. I cover with a second layer of cloth, then water gently. Set the container in a cool spot where it gets dim light. Water daily and within ninety days, you should have a flat of healthy, colorful moss.

If you live in a mild climate, try baby's-tears, a fast-growing cover you may want to consider as a seasonal planting if it does not survive winter. And take a look at ferns. There are many in good scale. Those that propagate by spores can be raised at home. These include the spleenworts, the brake ferns, and several polypody species.

Spores usually ripen in fall and turn rich brown when ready. To collect them, hold a piece of paper beneath a frond and tap gently. Sow the spores immediately or keep them under refrigeration until spring. I usually sow in March in a flat of peat, sand, and loam moistened until it is sponge-damp.

I tap the spores from the paper onto the soil in the flat, then cover with glass and place the flat at a north window. Soon the ferns come through, tiny green plants I can scarcely see. I let them grow until they are finger length, then prick them out, transferring the best to my bonsai.

Value of a Training Bed

Call them transplanting areas or training beds, but by any name reserve a section of your garden for unpotted bonsai. Use it as a hospital to renew sick trees, as a place to thicken young plants, and as a staging area for trees collected from the wild.

My plot is five by ten feet, spaded to a depth of two feet with peat and sand added. I don't include humus because I find it increases danger of infection for my wild trees, and I give them special treatment.

Often the most desirable wild specimens are those with poorest roots. To reduce shock and to speed recovery, I leave roots as long as possible. Conifers, especially pines, are planted with a root-ball, but deciduous trees can be handled as bare-root stock. I pack trees dug from the wild in a plastic bag; the humidity of the bag helps to save them.

Newly-collected trees need extra water since their root systems have been damaged. I make sure they get it two ways. I fill the planting holes with water before I set trees out in the bed. Then I build a dike around each trunk. The dike works like a saucer, and through the first two weeks, I often fill it with water.

When plants must be moved in full leaf, I've discovered I can minimize wilting with an antidesiccant—a liquid plastic that can be sprayed on leaves to reduce transpiration. Nurseries and hardware stores carry several brands, and instructions are given on each can.

I let the trees stay in my training bed a full year. Then, when new growth shows the next spring. I remove them, trim roots, and transfer to good-sized wooden tubs. Afterwards, roots are pruned yearly until they are small enough to fit a bonsai container.

If you make cuttings in spring, move them to your training bed by October. Plant two inches apart. Transfer to containers the second year.

Seedlings should not be started in an open bed—there they would develop overlong taproots. Instead start them in a flat and then transfer to the bed. A year there adds size and character, and many seedlings develop to *mame* size.

7. To Control Growth

Soon after I began growing bonsai, I discovered that the important techniques were hand arts. As I learned to control size, I realized how essential ten fingers could be. From early spring on, I had been pinching and nipping shoots. Now I was stripping leaves.

These finger skills are easy to master. Pinching and nipping, sometimes called "stopping," because they check new growth, encourage foliage and flower development, and regulate branch diameter as well. On some trees leaf-stripping or leaf-cutting is essential to reduce the size of leaves.

The theory behind this direct control is based on the fact that buds elongate into shoots; without controls, plant strength goes to the upper parts. Lower growth then weakens, often dies. Pinching the ends of shoots checks the upward flow of sap. With a twist of thumb and forefinger, you short-circuit it, sending it below to improve tone and health in the lower branches. As a rule, the earlier and more severe the pinching, the slower the tree grows and the smaller it stays.

Timing Controls The best time to check growth varies with each species, but in the temperate zones, it is usually in late March or early April. Then shoots are young, tender, and an inch or two long. Some evergreens, as the Japanese black pine and Yeddo spruce, produce new growth only once a year. Pinch these once and pinch them early. But many needle evergreens develop new growth in several spurts throughout the growing season. Start pinching them in April and continue as long as they continue to increase size. A few deciduous trees, as zelkova and the Japanese and trident maples, may need the same season-long attention.

Young trees often show bursts of growth from spring through fall.

Older bonsai may increase mostly, or only, in spring. On the majority, pinch new growth as it develops over a period of weeks. Remove the least vigorous buds first, then all but the most energetic, and last, those that grow best. This approach establishes good balance.

To Control Growth

Be wary of late-season growth, especially on deciduous and broadleaf trees. In fall, shoots are often sappy, and they detract from the shape of a tree. In some cases, the distance between nodes may be far enough to reduce strength and destroy branch appearance, so even in fall it may be necessary to check growth. As a rule, rub or pinch off adventitious shoots—those accidental, out-of-place pieces—at any time. However, if a shoot appears in an area that needs leaves, check its potential before you eliminate it. Sometimes unplanned new shoots are helpful and eventually produce interesting lines.

Pinching and nipping are techniques that should be adjusted to each species.

Pine Candles appear first, then needles and wood, the rate of growth varying with location. Candles in the upper branches grow first. To keep these short, nip the largest candle. Where there is a group, pinch out the center one. Nip the others later, as indicated. When growth seems too vigorous, remove one half or more of *each* candle. The amount depends on your purpose, since new growth will usually begin at the point at which you prune.

CONTROL FOR EVERGREENS

Japanese five-needle pine Pinch only when sprouts detract from shape. Indiscriminate pinching may result in loss of next year's foliage.

Cryptomeria, juniper, spruce, yew Trim repeatedly from April through midseason. Nip new growth when it is more than half an inch long. On many of these trees, buds develop first as balls then become shoots. Pinch when the balls begin to elongate. Grasp the new growth between thumb and forefinger and twist, leaving three to five whorls. At the height of the growing season, you may need to do this daily.

Sargent's juniper and some cypresses These continue growing into fall. Nip new buds as they appear, but do not pinch deeply. Deep pinching on Sargent's juniper, for example, can deform foliage. Avoid trimming plants recently collected from the wild. Pinching stimulates growth and newly transplanted trees need a full year's rest.

Trident maple, oak, zelkova Trim these early and continue into fall as development indicates. Start in April, cutting back new growth to one or two sets of leaves. Prune off late buds promptly unless one appears where you need a branch; then let it grow. Dense, twiggy trees should be pinched when new growth is an inch long.

CONTROL FOR DECIDUOUS TREES

Beech, elm, hornbeam, Japanese maple Unlike other maples, the Momiji or Japanese maple can be touchy. Young trees may be pinched

115

several times a season, but older ones often respond better to once-a-season stopping, and this early. With late trimming, branches often grow fast, and fast growth results in widely separated nodes. To shape-up beeches and elms properly, pinch them back often. In some cases, it also helps to leaf-cut early in the season to stimulate denser twig growth. Hornbeams are sturdy and can be shaped with shears.

FOR FLOWERING
AND FRUITING TREES

Don't work on these trees until they have stopped blooming. Buds that are forming need time to complete growth and you need to see them before you start pinching. Even after pinching, new shoots may appear. A few may produce blooms next year but they will be the exception. If pruning is done too early, especially on apricot, cherry, and quince, there will be little chance of flowers later. On the other hand, if trimming is delayed until shoots are hard, rather than tender, "summer suckers" may be produced, and these will not produce blooms. Flowering and fruiting trees are inclined to produce suckers on the trunk anyway. Remove them whenever you see them.

Techniques of pinching and nipping helped control size and shape of these Sawara cypresses. Peter Ioka.

To control size, pinch new growth with thumb and forefinger early in spring. Deadwood should not always be removed; on this Colorado spruce it has been developed over a three-year period. Peter Ioka.

A few growers warn against ever pinching such flowering shrubs as rose and jasmine, but I trim mine spring through fall. Most are active growers. I clip azaleas immediately after flowering with good results. New leaves develop wheel-like at the tips. I remove all but one or two in the cluster, and cut these back to two or three leaves.

Apple and pear bonsai are best pruned in fall after they lose leaves. But old or weak trees should not be pruned at all. Instead give them a light fertilizing and a period of rest. Pinch lightly the next year.

TO GET SMALLER LEAVES

If the leaves on your bonsai are in scale and if they produce fine fall color, let them alone. If the first leaves are oversized and unsightly or fall color is weak, then consider some leaf-cutting. It may give your bonsai a new look.

Most trees can lose the first round of foliage with safety and some, zelkova is one, can lose leaves as many as three times a season. They have "reserve buds," nature's insurance, a reservoir for the next year's growth. When you strip off the first leaves, the reserves are called into action. In a week or two, a healthy second crop appears. On most trees, the second growth is substantially smaller than the first, and on some, like the trident maple, second growth produces more vibrant autumn color.

There are several ways to force a second growth. You can strip the tree, pull off only alternate leaves, or clip each leaf in half. Method does not seem important so long as leaf stalks or petioles are not damaged. I've seen good results from each technique. A few trees, like the elm, can be cut back to dormant buds. These then become active and produce smaller leaves. Some growers use a similar technique on needle evergreens.

In some cases, leaf-cutting works another way. Trees with oversized leaves, like the oak, do not respond to stripping. It is better to remove half the leaves. Then there is more space around those that remain, and this makes leaves *appear* smaller. Sometimes foliage in certain areas of the tree will work visually as branches, and this helps to unify scale and design.

TO THICKEN
LIMBS AND TRUNKS

Limb-size is controlled by the amount of life each branch supports. The greater the number of leaves and small branches a limb carries, the bigger it will become because more nutrition is being channeled to it. Take advantage of this fact to help thicken undersized limbs. Let all possible growth remain on small limbs, even though, for the time, extra foliage detracts from appearance; also, open the area above to let in sun.

(*Above left*), Check an unplanned shoot in an open area before pinching it off; it may develop interesting new lines. The top of this collected cork oak has been pruned to reduce height, but a new leader will be trained. Peter Ioka. (*Right*), Avoid too early pruning that destroys flower buds on a species like this Japanese plum. Yoshio Sato. (*Below left*), This nandina was controlled by pinching. (*Right*), This received less control and is bushier and fuller. Dan Buckley.

Some growers remove foliage from a strong opposing limb on the theory that extra nutrition will then go to the sparser branch opposite because this will then carry proportionately more leaves. Others make a V-cut in the trunk below a small or weak branch. They maintain that the cut checks and then directs the flow to sap, thus stimulating growth on the branch above. I've never tired this, but the concept does make sense. After the weak branch develops adequate diameter, you can equalize foliage on the two branches.

Trunks can be thickened in much the same way. Promote growth of branches and foliage low on the trunk, for the more limbs that grow there, the thicker the trunk will become. As a rule, lower branches thicken the base, upper branches thicken the parts of the trunk directly below them.

You can add considerably to trunk diameter by transplanting a tree from a container to the open ground and letting it grow there for a year. The greater amount of soil promotes roots, and roots help to fatten a trunk. Girdling also works. Wrap a copper wire around the trunk *below* ground-level. The trunk directly above will soon swell and thicken. Then you must remove the wire to avoid dangerous constriction and a too-limited flow of sap for health.

Hard-barked trees, such as pines, can be thickened considerably by slitting. In this technique, outer bark is cut vertically for a distance of two inches or more. Henry Matsutani, a grower in Lafayette, California, taught me how to apply this trick to pines. He cut to the cambium layer with a razor blade to stimulate the flow of sap. The trunk bled slightly, and he did not protect the wound with tree paint. Within a year, the diameter of the trunk had increased substantially.

To Give the Look of Age

Even well-shaped, nicely-contoured trees can be made more interesting and attractive if they can also be given the look of age. This can be accomplished in several ways. Since the tips of conifers grow downward as a tree gets older, pinch tips on a young tree and then wire down the first new needles that grow. You may need to repeat this treatment yearly on pines, but be persistent. To add to the illusion, also trim the top. Topping checks conical growth and gives the impression that a tree has reached ultimate height.

The presence of deadwood suggests that a tree is old. Sometimes it is really the deadwood that makes a bonsai appear out of the ordinary. Natural deadwood can readily be dramatized; when none exists, it can be produced artificially.

To emphasize deadwood already present, peel off the bark. Work gently with razor blade or sharp knife. Then erase cut marks by smoothing wood with a cabinetmaker's scraper or a piece of glass. Or you can slit bark to the cambium layer, then peel it off. If you first dip the branches you wish to treat in hot water, it may make bark easier to peel.

The preferred deadwood is silver-white. In nature, this is a result of sun-bleaching. In bonsai, you can produce this effect artificially. For light breaching, apply a solution of lemon juice and water or of *diluted* Clorox. For a stronger, more dramatic effect, use a commercial furniture bleach. However, this usually has a pretty harsh effect, so experiment on a piece of detached wood before you apply it to a valuable bonsai.

Limb-size as on this wisteria is controlled by the amount of life it supports. To increase thickness, let more foliage remain.

(*Above*), This beautiful, thick twin-trunk ginkgo is living proof that size is considerably controlled by the life it supports. Courtesy, Dan Buckley. (*Below*), Trim spruce from April through midsummer. The clipping will smooth the edges and establish form as on this dwarf Alberta spruce.

8. How to Water Bonsai

Water is vital to plant growth. It expands the tissues and cells that keep a tree erect, and water carries nutrition. The amount a tree needs to keep alive, erect, and healthy depends on species, size, season—even on the container. A large bonsai, at the height of summer, may need two quarts a day; a *mame* in winter may need a pint a week. Dark soils and dark containers absorb more sun and evaporate moisture faster than those of lighter color.

TECHNIQUES OF WATERING

Japanese growers claim it takes three years to learn to water. Although this seems an exaggeratioin, it does illustrate the point that watering is an important technique, and one not quickly learned. The trick is to be consistent. Too little water causes wilting, damage to capillary roots and death. Too much water results in loss of aeration, "sour" soil, and consequent root rot. But if the potting mixture insures the proper drainage, frequency of watering then depends on only a few variables.

Trees like the willow require plenty of moisture and should be watered even when the soil is noticeably damp. Trees that prefer a dry condition, pine for example, should not be watered until the soil feels dry. Color can also be a guide, since soil lightens in color as moisture evaporates. Or scratch the surface. If the soil below looks rather dark, there is usually still enough moisture in it. Timing also depends on the nature of your plants, the containers, the climate. How to water properly must be learned by experience.

WHEN TO WATER

Through winter a watering schedule from once a day to once a week may be adequate. If you live in a very cold climate, take care not to overwater. Cool soil retains moisture longer than warm soil. If freezing temperatures are common, overwatering invites disaster—broken containers and damaged trees.

124

In spring, the amount of water is especially important. Too much makes trees grow too fast. Leaves get large, growth becomes soft, long, and disjointed. You can protect plants against excessive rain with plastic skirts wrapped around trunks. Extend the plastic out over the rim of the container.

Speed up the schedule in summer. Then most plants require watering once or twice a day, pines usually only once. A few, especially rock plantings and *mame,* may need it three times. In fall, as temperatures decline and humidity rises, watering can be decreased. I water most plants daily when it is sunny, two or three times a week when it is cloudy. *Mame* are watered once a day even in winter.

You can water bonsai at almost any hour of day but if you can, water at the same time each day, for container plants adapt to routine. Morning is probably the best time, although many businessmen water their bonsai after work in the evenings.

Bonsai should be soaked immediately after potting, then let rest for a day or longer before receiving more water. The interval allows newly-pruned roots to adapt to changed conditions; the length of the interval depends upon the severity of the pruning. In no case should a tree go more than three days without water. After the second post-potting watering, put your bonsai on a regular schedule.

Some growers soak plants in a tub with the water level at three-fourths the height of the container. Others submerge the pot, the water level then being above the soil. Either technique is satisfactory, so long as soil is thoroughly moistened. Plastic tubs make good portable soakers. Permanent tubs for soaking can be made from redwood or cedar boards, lined with fiber glass and secured with liquid plastic (resin), or old porcelain basins and tubs can be used. I have a laundry tub near my potting bench.

Another method consists of daily watering with a can or hose. Most desirable is a gentle spray that will neither disturb nor erode soil. Many gardeners use a watering can, considering it safest. Good ones, in metal or plastic, are available from nurseries, and a few specialists still offer the beautiful, long-necked copper cans that Japanese growers use. I prefer these because the Japanese rose or perforated nozzle delivers a softer spray.

The objection to the garden hose has been the difficulty of controlling the force of the water. In the past, it has been almost impossible to get a safe mist at low pressure. Now, several manufacturers offer a variety of nozzles and heads. In summer I water most of my collection with a hose that has a fine-spray nozzle. If you use a hose, be sure to let the sun-warmed water flow out of the hose *before* you spray your trees.

125

Soaking and spraying are the two basic watering techniques. Soaking is used immediately after potting and intermittently thereafter; you can build a soaker such as this from a porcelain sink.

126

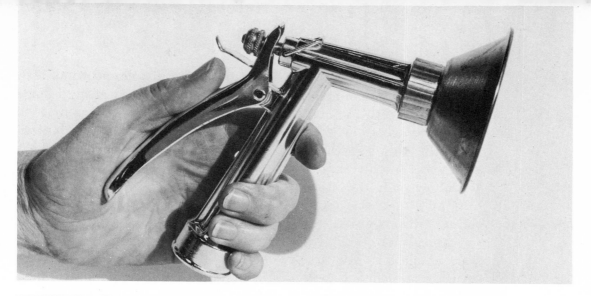

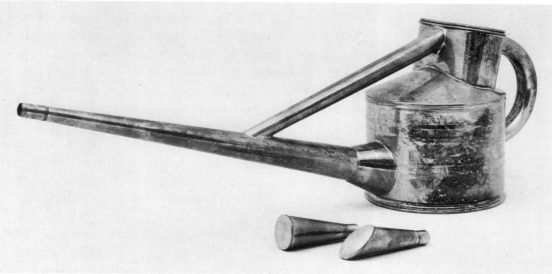

(*Top*), An attachment like this with a good "rose" or spray nozzle delivers a fine, soft shower. (*Center*), American-type watering cans do nicely, but many growers favor this Japanese design. (*Below*), Misting, so important in summer, can be accomplished with an insect-sprayer or a mechanic's tool, like this one.

Try this two-step technique. Direct the water at soil and trunk first. Fill the container completely. Then water from above, wetting foliage as well as soil. Fill the container a second time. Two fillings may be adequate but check whether moisture is seeping through the bottom drains—the only sign that a plant has had enough water. But don't underwater. Too little water causes roots to reach toward the surface, and shallow roots are susceptible to sunburn.

RAINWATER Exacting growers insist on rainwater, but aside from the fact that such soft water is more quickly absorbed, insistence on rainwater seems to me an affectation. Admittedly, chlorinated water is not the best for bonsai, but the chemicals in most city supplies are not harmful. Many good bonsai have been raised on city water. If salts collect, remove them from the soil by leaching, that is, flushing through, once or twice a year. Although the temperature of water is hardly a critical matter, water should not be much warmer or colder than soil and air.

These general techniques work for most plants, but some respond better with special attention in the matter of water. Cryptomeria, for example, likes moisture. Give it plenty of water through summer, and plant a ground-cover to retain surface moisture. Take care not to over-water the cherry; overwatering may cause loss of branches. To minimize development of sappy growth on trees that bloom on old wood, as apricot and crabapple, water them less at the time buds are forming. If fruit trees blossom in rainy weather, cover the flowers with plastic.

ABOUT MISTING Misting, the wetting of foliage by spray, is important in summer. Misting makes up for water lost through leaves by evaporation, increases humidity, and helps the stoma—the mouthlike openings on the leaves —to expand and so reduce leaf temperature. Rely on misting to remove any soot, dust, or chemicals that may collect on foliage. These can interfere with photosynthesis—the process by which chlorophyll is used with light to manufacture food in the form of sugars and starches.

Mist bonsai in the morning, and again in the evening, in hot weather. The moisture-loving species also benefit from a midday misting as well. Don't mist trees in winter if freezing temperatures are a possibility. Misting can be deadly then.

To make watering easier, keep the soil-level below the rim of the container as in this planting of a cork oak. Peter Ioka.

When roots force plants to set high in the container as with this Japanese maple, space can still be kept around the rim to receive water, but watering will be mainly accomplished by spraying the mounded roots several times a day. Peter Ioka.

130

9. To Protect from Weather, Pest, and Disease

Seasonal extremes can have a most adverse affect on bonsai, for container plants cannot tolerate the range of conditions their relatives in open ground accept. However, with surprisingly little protection, you can keep most bonsai safe and healthy the year-round.

Warm days and hot sun can be good for your trees. In moderation the combination makes bonsai broader, shorter, and sturdier. But too much sun is harmful, and shade is most important to avoid wilting and leaf burn.

SUMMER PROTECTION

If you have just a few trees, set them on a table under a shade tree or display them beside a fence or building where they receive only part-day sun. Morning sun is best, if there is a choice. And keep in mind that the light-colored wall of a nearby structure can reflect a tremendous amount of sunshine.

What to do with plants that require daily care when you go on vacation? The answer depends on the size of your collection and the length of time you'll be away. Short trips are seldom a problem. You can easily handle bonsai so they will survive a two- or three-day weekend. Put them in shade. Water them thoroughly at the last possible moment, then cover the soil with damp newspaper, burlap, or moss. If you live in a low-humidity area, as in parts of the Southwest, place buckets of water near the plants. The increased humidity will reduce evaporation. In the case of moisture-loving trees like willow that need extra water, stand the containers right in water before you leave.

VACATION CARE

Longer trips require more planning. Small collections can be boarded at a local nursery, also the valuable plants of a large collection. If you'd rather not move your bonsai about, consider hiring a local

131

gardener or a neighbor. If you work out—and type out—a careful, exact schedule, even untrained help, if reliable, can do a good job. But you won't need help if you install overhead sprinklers. Clock-operated, they turn on and off automatically.

Give extra protection to trees in small containers. *Mame* and youngsters in liners can be placed—in their containers—in a seed flat filled with soil. The extra earth will hold moisture longer than the small amount in the pots. Bonsai that might otherwise require two or three waterings a day can survive on one, and getting someone to water once a day is within the realm of possibility, two or three times, probably not.

WINTER PROTECTION

Even the hardiest trees grown as bonsai need special winter care, and you can provide this better if you know their hardiness ratings and moisture requirements.

If yours is a temperate climate, trees may need nothing more than protection from rain. Heavy rains, especially in spring, can stimulate startling, unexpected growth. If rains are only occasional, some temporary shelter will be adequate. Wrap plastic skirts around the trunks, below the foliage, then extend the plastic a little beyond the container so as to completely cover the soil. If long periods of rain or snow are likely to occur, build a permanent shelter. A simple stand will suffice.

Use 2-by-2's for corner posts with a 1-by-2 framework across the top. Set the frame over your bonsai, then cover it with wood, plastic, or glass. Add a back and two sides and you've provided a shelter from wind. If trees are enclosed on three sides, give them a southern exposure. Rotate plants in the shelter so that foliage gets an equal amount of sun. Of course, just one tree can be protected by placing an inverted box over it.

Frost is the serious problem for it can seriously damage plants. Also, bonsai containers are small, and even a light freeze may break them. A coldframe gives the best protection. Set in plants at the first sign of freezing weather, and remove them as early as possible in spring. It is not wise to let new growth mature in a coldframe because it cannot be properly "seasoned" there. Watering is rarely needed in a coldframe, certainly not more than two or three times a winter at the most.

TO BUILD A COLD FRAME

If you don't have a coldframe, consider building one. The simplest arrangement is nothing more than four walls and a transparent roof. In dry areas a flat roof is permissible but where there is much rain, a sloping top is essential. Make the coldlframe any size you wish. If you work in multiples of three by six feet, you will be building to standard nursery size and can use conventional nursery sash, a glass top superior to others.

Use 1-by-12 or 2-by-12 boards for the walls. To resist rot and borers, insist on redwood, cedar, cypress, or treated fir. Excavate a plot, the size of your frame, fifteen to thirty inches below ground-level, then erect the walls inside the hole. If you build your own top, make it as simple or as complicated as you like. I made the frame on mine of 2-by-2 lumber and covered the two sides with plastic. You can add a backing of wire-mesh to the plastic to carry a snow-load.

Place five to ten inches of river rock on the ground inside the frame. Your bonsai will set on this. If more protection than the frame is needed, mulch plants with straw, moss, or bark.

Trees that are not wintered in a coldframe, can be dug in outside. Where near-zero weather is likely, remove them from their pots to keep containers from breaking, mulch with straw, bark, or moss for extra protection.

Seedlings, newly-grafted stock, and trees collected from the wild need special care when they are first transplanted. Shade them from direct sun and shelter them from wind to give them a chance to stiffen, root, and take hold. To shade several plants, make a low-level, temporary lath house. A four-foot square should protect twelve to sixteen plants. If you have a coldframe, build the panel to the size of the frame. It can then do double duty.

Wind is particularly harmful to recent transplants. Their root systems are small, and even a light breeze increases evaporation of moisture from leaves faster than the roots can replace it. If you have only a few plants, you can make individual windbreaks for them. For small trees, use shingles, cardboard, even sections of milk cartons. For many plants, you can make a more permanent arrangement by tacking cloth, canvas, or plastic to stakes driven into the corners of a bed.

Bonsai are rarely attacked by pests or disease, probably because they are so closely watched and we all wing into action at the first sign of trouble. Each species grown as a bonsai is, of course, susceptible to the same pests and diseases as the plant grown under more natural conditions. If trouble is suspected, specific information should be sought in a book devoted to the species, but, as a rule, it can be averted by regular application of some commercial all-purpose dust or spray (always diluted more than recommended) or the use of a simple formula like this one of mine. I make it of calcium oxide and sulphur—a pinch of each to a gallon of water. Dilute 25 to 1, and spray on all but such delicate trees as cherry. Materials can be obtained from some drugstores; mine comes from a chemical-supply house.

Earthworms are a menace because their burrowings upset drainage. To get rid of them, apply a worm-repellent to the soil, repot and keep containers from contact with the ground.

133

Container plants cannot tolerate the range of conditions their relatives in open ground accept. A lath house provides protection and a place for display. John A. Dutro.

134

Concrete piers as corner-post supports, and concrete blocks as shelf bases limit the transfer of insects. Peter Ioka.

Plants in small containers can be placed in flats of soil; the earth will hold extra moisture and plants that might otherwise need two waterings a day can get along with one.

(*Above*), Make the top of 2 by 2's and cover with glass or use two layers of plastic sheeting, as I do here. (*Below*), For circulation, prop up the top on warm days; be sure to close at night.

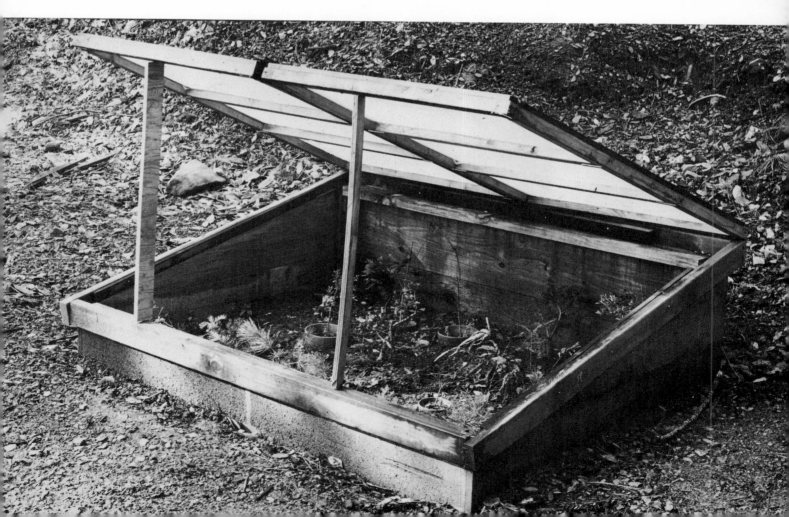

If your trees need only rain protection to prevent flooding, cover soil with a plastic skirt. Cut a sheet of plastic larger than the container and pin or tape it around the trunk, below foliage, above soil.

138

Training beds where plants can be heeled-in provide a measure of winter protection. If freezing weather is likely, remove containers before placing bonsai. Add mulch for extra protection.

139

Surface fertilizers may attract pests. Rapeseed cake, for example, may harbor insects that lay eggs under the meal. DDT or nicotine will control them, but you can usually get rid of insects by easier means. Summer misting helps to control leaf insects. Plenty of sun and air will often kill eggs. Most important is good plant health. A strong bonsai can almost fight its own battles.

Watch out for slugs; they often take shelter under bonsai pots. Lift pots to check from time to time. To protect seedlings, sprinkle slug bait around them.

To get rid of cutworms, particularly in your training bed, surround young plants with tar-paper disks or collars made from milk cartons.

But most of the ills of bonsai are due to physiological conditions—poor nutrition, impacted drainage, too much sun or rain or cold. In the chart below are outlined *some* of the conditions that may bother you, their probable causes, and hopefully, remedies for them.

Problems and Solutions

Symptoms	Possible causes	Remedies to try
Plant as a whole		
Unusually slow top growth	Nutritional deficiency, or hard-packed, waterlogged soil.	Repot in a fresh soil mixture with good drainage arrangements. For possible sulphur deficiency, add ammonium sulphate, flowers of sulphur, or lime sulphur to soil, all available from garden centers.
Wilting of plants	Excessive evaporation of moisture from leaves due to prolonged exposure to sun or wind; to root damage, or to sudden temperature change as when a plant displayed inside, is returned outside.	Place in shade; check and treat roots if damaged in repotting; apply disease controls if required.
Wilting of seedlings	Probably damping-off, a fungus disease.	Prick out affected seedlings, perhaps discard all; next time sow in disinfected soil or perlite.
Dull, rusty appearance	Probably a fungus attack.	Isolate affected trees; apply a general fungicide, a specific one if necessary.
Weak areas, some with smaller leaves	Sun not reaching whole; insects in roots.	Rotate position; sometimes health of one branch can be improved by sacrificing another in the same

Problems and Solutions

Symptoms	Possible causes	Remedies to try
		area, or by reducing the number of leaves or twigs on the ailing branch. Inspect roots and if insects are present, apply a general or specific soil insecticide; and consider repotting.
Late dormancy or none	Too much heat and light.	Change gradually to a more natural environment; don't try to "force" bonsai into bloom.

Leaves and branches

Symptoms	Possible causes	Remedies to try
Leaves, yellow	Chlorosis—iron deficiency —may be due to a leaching away of natural iron, lack of iron in soil, or compounds that make iron insoluble; occurs most often in alkaline soils.	Add iron chelates available for soil or foliar feeding; or lay rusty nails or iron chunks on the soil.
Leaves, brown	Blight (leafspot), or roots too small to help plant make up evaporation lost through leaves.	Apply fungicide for blight.
Leaves, burned	Too much sun, likely to damage maple.	Put plant in shade; harden new growth in spring by gradually exposing to sun; don't fertilize until leaves harden. If considerable burn, defoliate tree entirely; new growth will appear. If second growth burns don't defoliate again. Try to improve health of plant and avoid overexposure to sun next season.
Leaves, shriveled	Wind, especially after a period of rain or sun; or misting with very cold water.	Move to sheltered spot in shade, especially during hot part of day. Mist with *tepid* water.
Evergreen needles too long	Overwatering early in growing season.	Reduce water and expose to more sun.
Poor fall color	Overwatering earlier in season or nutritional deficiency.	Next year, strip tree once in spring; grow in full sun; feed.

141

Problems and Solutions

Symptoms	Possible causes	Remedies to try
Buds, Fruits, Flowers		
Dying branches	Unhealthy roots; poor drainage.	Repot in a fresh soil mixture and assure proper drainage; remove branch, or if important to design, retain as deadwood and consider bleaching.
Slow flowering and fruiting	Nutritional deficiency or insects.	Improve soil but don't fertilize while buds are forming; try adding boron to soil; spray for insects.
Failure to bloom	Disease, inadequate root development, too early pruning that removed buds, natural slowness of seedlings as some dogwood that take up to seven years.	Balance foliage to roots by judiciously cutting back tops.

10. Containers-
How to Select Them

Much of the pleasure of bonsai lies in selecting containers, for very beautiful ones can be obtained from bonsai specialists, garden shops, and importers, who will even order special shapes and colors for you. You can also make your own containers from clay or wood, or use boxes, cans, or iron vessels not originally intended for bonsai but still suitable.

For practical containers at practical prices, modern bonsai pots are not only good buys but handsome as well. Sets of three sell for less than five dollars, and even old-time growers like them. Most of us select containers for their appearance, and recently cliques have sprung up in the world of bonsai who vociferously favor specific manufacturers, as Tokoname, Satsuma, Imari, Kutani, and some six other Japanese producers.

Of course, very old containers are prized. Chinese pots are the rarest and most expensive, and a few wealthy American growers collect Kowatari containers the way the British collect Oriental porcelains. The best Kowatari are more than two hundred years old, and worth thousands of dollars each. Shinwatari (Shinto) pots, made in China for the Japanese market between 1910 and 1920, are also popular. Though less rare, they still sell for several hundred dollars apiece—if and when they can be found. If you have an opportunity to see fine old Chinese pots by all means do so. They have a special beauty, a patina not found in any other containers.

A bonsai container, old or new, plays a double role. It functions as a picture frame defining and limiting a composition in an artistic setting. It also has the practical purpose of providing a means of holding and draining soil. The finish of a pot, glazed or unglazed, affects both looks and health.

144

(*Left*), Chinese containers have become collector's items, worth thousands of dollars. Even newer ones, such as this modified oval, holding a Chinese quince, are sought after for their patina. Collection of Dan Buckley. (*Above*), Reserve decorated containers for dramatic trees like this. Yoshio Sato.

ESSENTIAL REQUIREMENTS

Drains. A proper bonsai container must have at least one drain, and larger ones should have two or more. A few pots are made without holes. They are designed for bonkei or saikei—miniature landscapes—and rock plantings, and should not be used for bonsai unless drains are drilled.

Be sure the bottom of a container is flat, to facilitate drainage. Inexpensive pots may have grooved or uneven bases, even ridges around the drains. Avoid these, unless you plan to smooth the base. A good container does not retain water.

Finish In general an unglazed pot is more often used for bonsai than one with a glaze. Unglazed, it admits air to the soil, retains moisture, and absorbs some water through its walls, and the subtle texture is most pleasing with plants. However, pots with an outside glaze are desirable for some trees, a showy plum, for example, particularly when it is in bloom. But don't plant in a container with an inside glaze. Water is likely to stand in such a pot and a stagnant condition results. *Mame* containers are the exception because they are so small. In warm climates, glazing may even be healthful for *mame,* reducing the moisture loss of evaporation.

ARTISTIC CONSIDERATIONS

Color Most containers made for bonsai are in earthen tones, reds and browns, and these are always safe colors to use, associating naturally with the soil and appropriate for all trees. Somewhat darker hues are also good, contrasting gently with foliage and never intrusive.

Medium-red containers set off many conifers; lighter reds are better for junipers. Browns are good with pines, spruce, and maple. In fact, if I were to limit myself to one color it would be a rather dark brown. This is especially pleasing when contrasted to a rich green groundcover.

More colorful containers, blues and purples, yellows to whites, must be carefully considered; they can easily compete with a plant, or overwhelm it entirely. However, sky-blue usually enhances a maple and medium-blue a tree with dark red flowers, like the Japanese plum or flowering crabapple. Celadon or sea-green is good with ivy and ginkgo. White and off-white pots are for plants with pastel blossoms like a pale pink azalea. For apricot and quince light yellow pots are traditional, and celadon is another possibility.

Shape Shapes can also be recessive or aggressive. Simple designs do not conflict with the design of a tree. But for a dramatic plant, a bright-colored flowering quince perhaps, a "petal" or flower container will be attractive.

The number of different containers is amazing. My Tokoname catalogue includes fifty pages of possibilities. Dan Buckley, an authority on containers, has even classified them as:

1 Square	5 Modified rectangular
2 Rectangular	6 Modified oval
3 Circular	7 Modified circular (petal or
4 Oval	flower shape)

"The Japanese have still more specific categories, like *dohimo,* which means a container with a belt," Buckley says, "and even these seven groups can be subdivided. For example, there are those with rolled rims, reversed edges, and incised lips. Corners have to be taken into account. They have dramatic value. Reversed and rolled corners are 'active,' straight edges, 'passive,' and aside from appearance, we have to admit that containers with constricted tops are more difficult to plant than straight-sided pots."

While containers are made to stand above the table as insurance for drainage, some pots are leggier than others. The legs can be simple bars, unobtrusive cloud shapes, or ornate feet. Tall legs add unnecessary height, and elaborate legs of any height may compete with both pot and tree.

The shape of a container relates to the height and to the spread of a bonsai. When the height of a tree is to be emphasized, square, circular, or modified circular containers are good choices. A tree in formal style is set off by a square or round pot. A tree with a slender trunk looks natural in a shallow circular container. Multiple plantings are effective in circular, petal, or hexagonal pots. Cascades are nearly always well displayed in square or circular pots that are taller than wide.

When the span of branches is more important than the height of a bonsai, use a rectangular, oval, modified rectangular, or modified oval pot. A deep, rectangular pot is excellent for a tree of dramatic form; a rectangular or oval container, for an off-center styling. Groves and forests are nicely balanced, in long, shallow rectangles and ovals, the shape depending on the height and width of grove or forest. Rock plantings seem at home in shallow or medium-depth containers.

(*Above*), Containers glazed on the outside but not inside are suitable for many plants. (*Below*), Unglazed containers like these of Tokoname ware are recommended because their porosity is usually healthful for plants. Imported by Dan Buckley.

(*Top*), When the branch spread is an important dimension, rectangular and oval containers look best. These sets are inexpensive. (*Center*), Here are six *mame* containers, glazed and unglazed, from Tokoname, imported by Dan Buckley. (*Below*), Three containers.

(*Above*), A container of strong, dramatic form suits a slender tree or a multiple-trunk planting. (*Below*), Legs and corners are important in a design. Incised rims are effective but containers with constricted openings are more difficult to use in transplanting. Imported by Dan Buckley.

When you want something unique, make it yourself. Many bonsai enthusiasts do. Visiting a dozen Western shows, I was impressed by the number of homemade clay and wooden containers I saw. I tried my first of clay after I saw a charming grove of dwarf bamboo in such a one. Mine was not so professional, but I keep trying.

I find wooden containers easier to make, and they are certainly popular. The simplest are shallow four-sided boxes with a nailed-on base. The better ones have mitered corners, fitted legs, and a weathered finish.

Why not try your hand at this? Wood is an excellent material for bonsai, porous, and increasingly attractive with age. Redwood, cedar, and cypress are all good, since they resist moisture, but almost any wood that weathers well can be used.

Bob Krohn, of the Marin Bonsai Club, is an expert on these wooden containers. He teaches woodworking at a high school in San Rafael, California, and has made hundreds of containers. "Corners give the most trouble," he says, "but they shouldn't. Make them mitered, butted, or dadoed, that is, set into grooves. Technique doesn't matter so long as you strengthen corners with waterproof glue or galvanized nails."

Bob makes containers with various kinds of bases. Some are nailed, some fitted to rabbeted sides, and some, interestingly, are removable. He says, "These are training pots; I add gussets, triangular inserts, to the corners, and leave the bottom boards loose. It makes repotting easier."

Bob applies various finishes, stains, and shellac. I saw beautiful weathered cedar containers that he had let silver naturally.

I have finished several pots with my own version of the ancient Japanese burnt-wood technique. Once the container is assembled, I go over the wood with a butane torch, then rub off the charred layer with a wire brush. The result is a raised grain and a dark finish, the color depending on the amount of brushing. To keep fingers clean, I finally wax or shellac the surface.

Unusual containers can also be "found." Boxes, cans, and cups made for other purposes can often be planted. A pickle-barrel cut in half provided two sections for rock plantings, a rectangular iron vessel from an antique shop made a handsome container for a beautiful Japanese boxwood. Such iron pieces can usually be found in the Chinatown section of any large city. Most of them have no holes but you can have them drilled. With time, a soft rusty patina develops.

Then there are ceramic pieces from low vases to antique pots. A collector of porcelain discovered a square sake cup years ago; she had it drilled, and now uses it for a five-inch *mame* Japanese maple.

The variety of containers for bonsai is almost unlimited. The imaginative collector finds them everywhere. So long as they do not compete with a tree in color, shape, or design, they are suitable.

When you want something special, consider making it yourself. This grove of bamboo, *Sasa pygmea,* is planted in a ceramic container made by Robert and Helen Woodward.

A naturally weathered wooden container with mitered corners enhances this bonsai. Mrs. Emil Steinegger.

154

Barnacles were acquired when this container was aged in the ocean.

(*Above*), Wood is a good medium for training pots. These, designed by Bob Krohn, have removable lower sections to make repotting easier. (*Below left*), Waterproof plywood from Holland is used for these straight-sided containers with three-quarter-inch drains, also built by Bob Krohn. (*Right*), A corner construction with a dado-cut is difficult but strong and good looking; a dowel inserted from the top, holds pieces together. Mrs. Emil Steinegger.

The shape of this wooden container on feet echoes the form of the dwarf Alberta spruce. Mrs. Emil Steinegger.

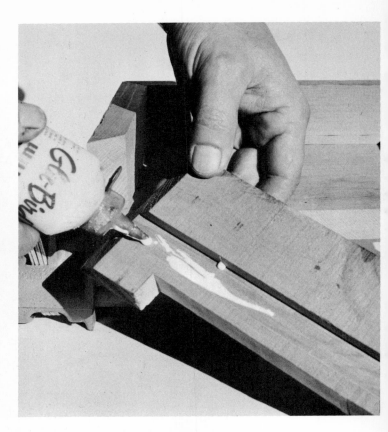

(*Above left*), Build to traditional measurements, if you like, with height one-third length, width two-thirds length. (*Right*), Use moisture-resistant cedar, redwood, or cypress, and assemble with waterproof glue or galvanized nails. (*Below left*), Fit pieces tightly together; if you glue, assemble with clamps. (*Right*), Here wood is charred with a butane torch, then rubbed with a wire brush to produce the burnt finish often used in the Orient.

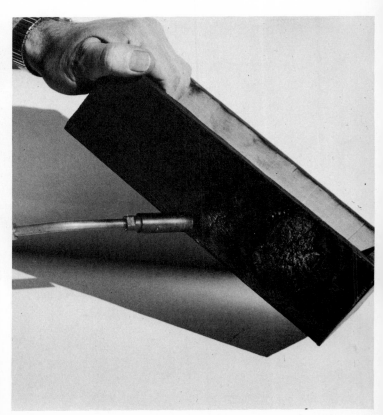

11. Tools, Clubs, Exhibitions and Importing

Here is a miscellany of information for reference on tools, display areas, clubs and shows, and importing.

Tools

Until you have a number of plants, you can get by with just a few tools. I started with a pair of shears, a pair of pliers, and a trowel.

For pruning and training Let one pair of shears do double duty. The best are Japanese, and made just for bonsai. They are flat faced, come in several sizes, and are designed to make concave cuts, a most desirable feature. Buy a pair that will cut branches the size of your thumb.

If you can't obtain Japanese shears, buy one of the hook-and-blade cutters made here. I find these superior to the anvil type because they make a cleaner cut. Add a pair of needle-nosed pliers for wiring, several gauges of copper wire, and a ball of twine for tie-downs, and you will have a basic pruning and training kit. Flush-jaw cutters clip copper wire closer and more safely than pliers or diagonal cutters.

For potting and watering Essentials are: a trowel, sifting screens (two or more ¼-inch to ⅟₃₂-inch mesh), a 12-by-12-inch square of drain screen and tin snips to cut it, a watering can, and a sprayer for misting leaves (a hand-operated insect sprayer works well).

Eventually you will want some specialized tools. Japanese-designed kits can be purchased for less than twenty dollars, or you can buy this useful equipment piece by piece:

1 Three or more shears in assorted sizes for buds, leaves, and hard-to-prune areas.
2 Pincers for heavy-duty wire.
3 Pincers for thick branches and roots.
4 Lazy Susan pruning table bought or made.
5 Cutting knives or woodworking tools for smoothing, trimming, and shaping pruning wounds and deadwood.
6 "Pinchettes" for removing dead leaves and pressing the soil around the edges of a pot; good ones have a small, trowel-like end.
7 Soft fiber whisk broom for smoothing the surface of the soil.

159

For collecting To make this easier, you need lightweight tools. My kit includes a hand ax, folding saw, and shovel, burlap, twine, sphagnum moss, water jug, plastic bags, and a small pack frame. With this equipment, I can bring back almost any tree. I include a small pick for working in a rocky area.

Work Centers

A permanent work area reduces confusion and helps to avoid contamination. If you are serious about bonsai—and we all seem to become so —do consider building a convenient work center. Almost any corner will do. A San Francisco enthusiast adapted part of her display bench, covering it with galvanized tin (an excellent work surface) and providing storage space below. Another built a counter against a back fence, adding shelves and sliding doors beneath. He uses the top for potting, pruning, and training. The storage protects tools, containers, and soils from weather, and the doors keep his yard neat.

Make your bench at least 3-by-5 feet, and waist high so you can work without bending. Put in a sturdy shelf below for heavy storage, a smaller one above for chemicals. If you include a drawer, you can store tools more conveniently. Buy plastic cans to hold potting mixes. Adding on a roof will give you shade if not all-weather protection.

Display Areas

It increases the pleasure of growing bonsai if you have a place to view them properly, a spot for your own seasonal shows—blossoms in spring, rich coloring in fall. Outdoors you can group a few around your patio or pool, but a collection deserves a special provision, perhaps a series of free-standing shelves made of 1-by-12's laid over concrete blocks or attached to a structure, a house or garage wall. Here the effect of heat radiation and light reflection must be taken into account. Of course, shelves on multiple levels will display your bonsai to fine advantage. If you attach wooden supports, place them on concrete piers or flagstones to discourage ants and slugs. Japanese growers often sink supports, especially metal ones, in water.

To guard against pots tipping over in wind, secure tall containers, particularly pots of cascades to the shelves. Bands of rubber cut from inner tubes and slipped over pots and around shelves work best. Indoors, bonsai can be safely displayed only for a brief time, in summer for two or three days; in winter for four or five. In Japan the traditional *tokonoma* or alcove, a part of every house, makes a lovely setting for, usually, but one bonsai at a time. Since they are miniatures, they look best in a space that does not crowd them nor emphasize their small scale, and in a setting of suitable color. The Japanese reserve certain background colors for formal display, for example, gold screens to enhance their pines and apricots. Most trees are well set off by solid colors—tans, whites, and grays—and colored cardboard can be used.

Brilliant colored and patterned wallpaper may prove overwhelming. In Japan, decorative scrolls and watercolors are often added, but with us, the effect seems to lose in translation.

Bonsai Clubs

Membership in a bonsai club gives you a chance to learn and to enjoy the companionship of other enthusiasts, and clubs exist or are springing up everywhere with more than a hundred at this time in the United States alone. New York City has two, the Greater New York Bonsai Society being one of the nation's oldest. Two clubs in Florida—the Miami Bonsai Club and the Gold Coast Bonsai Club—hold joint three-day workshops every year. In the San Francisco area, seven clubs hold regular meetings. There are also active clubs in Cincinnati, Chattanooga, Dallas, and more than fifty other cities. There are large, active clubs in Canada, England, Germany, and South Africa.

Bonsai Clubs International is becoming a clearing house for research, information, and club addresses. A yearly convention is held in San Francisco, usually in February, and this is well attended by growers from many parts of the world. A newer organization, the American Bonsai Society, has been formed on the East Coast with similar objectives as well as the purpose of developing representative "American" bonsai. This society also holds yearly conventions. Addresses of both groups are given under Sources at the end of the book.

If you join a club, you will be sure to show your trees publicly, for most clubs have at least one exhibition a year. In Japan, one of the biggest is held in January at the Mitsukoshi department store in Tokyo. In February, the Kikufu Bonsai Association puts on its famous show at the Ueno Art Musuem; the June Azalea Show is held in Hibiya Park in the heart of Tokyo.

Exhibiting

Here, as in Japan, display benches and backgrounds are provided by the show committee. You'll be given adequate space for your plants, and you'll be responsible for their display. Large bonsai can be shown on a bench but smaller trees look better if raised.

Show your trees in spotless containers on stands that dramatize them. If you have hard-to-clean unglazed containers, try floor wax instead of soap. Add rocks and mats for atmosphere, but don't let them be important enough to compete with your bonsai. I have seen a handsome Norway spruce effectively displayed against an antique miniature screen, and I have admired three trees dramatically silhouetted against a bamboo mat and an open fan.

In other countries, exhibitions are held only for viewing pleasure but here many shows are competitive. Trees are judged on the basis of style, form, and in various other categories. In some classes, trees are rated on conformity to traditional standards, in others artistic freedom is al-

161

lowed. As yet, there is no accepted standard of evaluation, but at a recent state fair, bonsai were judged on this basis:

Horticultural perfection	20 percent
Scale	20 percent
Form	20 percent
Age and rarity	20 percent
Artistic effect of tree and container	20 percent

The safest means of transporting bonsai to a show is in your car. If you can actually tie the container to the car almost any bonsai will ride safely. On long trips, place a tree in a wooden box, and tie the container to the bottom of the box. One exhibitor does this and then fills the box with sand, working it gently around the branches. The sand acts as a shock absorber, the only drawbacks being weight and the fact that the sand must be removed when the plant is watered.

Importing   Seventy-five species of bonsai can be readily imported, twenty come in under a delayed quarantine, but more than twenty—including certain maples, plums, and bamboos—cannot be brought in at all. When you want a plant from another country, the best way is to get a professional grower, here or abroad, to get it for you. He knows the routine and will have proper permits. However, if you want to import, get in touch with the United States Department of Agriculture, request a list of acceptable plants, and also Plant Quarantine Form No. 546 and No. 687.

Japanese kits are available from many sources and experienced growers prefer them. These two shears are recommended for beginners.

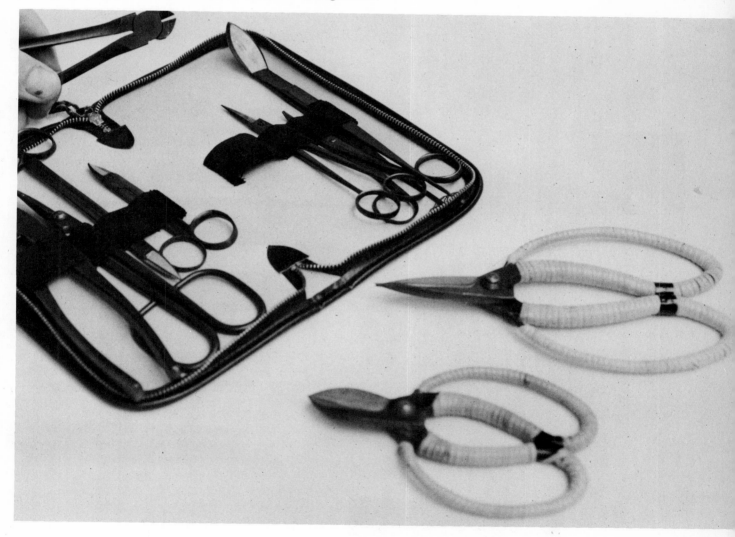

Grafting kit includes knives and cutters that are also useful for layering and cutting.

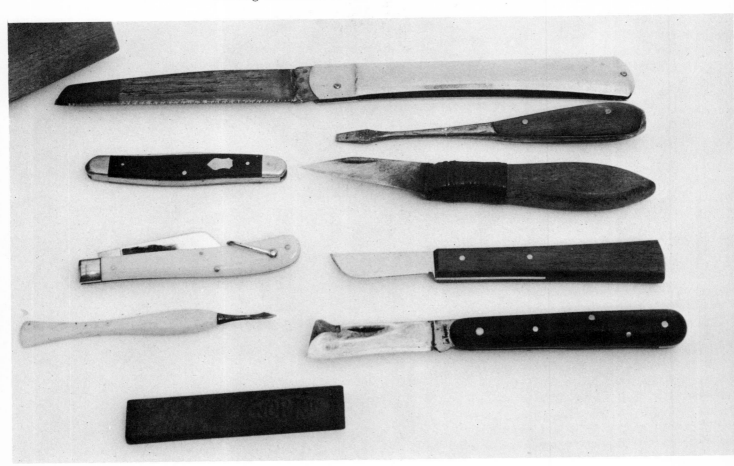

Lazy Susan bench, a work top on casters, is most useful and can be bought ready-made, or you can build one like this of Don Croxton's.

A bench of 2 by 12 cedar, set off by a bamboo fence, makes a simple but effective outdoor display area.

A slat fence forms an interesting background, and attached shelves hold a good-sized collection. This one offers an imaginative approach—individual niches for pots. Mrs. Emil Steinegger.

167

(*Above*), A log stand, and (*below*) a stand made from a root keep displays in character with the unfinished design of the area. John A. Dutro.

Cascade bonsai are effective displayed on formal stands.

(*Above*), As a rule, benches are provided by the show committee. Exhibitions use backgrounds of paper or cloth panels. Large bonsai are set directly on benches, smaller trees elevated on stands. From an American Bonsai Society show. (*Below*), Most clubs hold at least one exhibition a year, such as this show sponsored by the American Bonsai Society.

12. Grove and Rock Plantings

Grove, group, and forest bonsai may look difficult but they are not; their dramatic effect simply makes them appear so. Actually these are among the easiest of all bonsai. "There is safety in numbers," I tell beginners, "if you want bonsai that are beautiful but undemanding, try the multiples."

Not long ago Jack A. Dutro, founder of California's East Bay Bonsai Club, noticed that none of his club's one hundred members planned to enter a grove in an upcoming show. "There should be at least one," Jack insisted.

He gathered a handful of Japanese cedar seedlings from his training bed and went to work. In less than an hour Jack had what he wanted—a delightful forest set on a rolling slope. After the soil was covered with fresh green moss, the bonsai had a settled, permanent look. While it was not entered in competition, it certainly could have been. "The so-called difficult plantings are like this," Jack said. "You enjoy them immediately. Groves are the original no-wait bonsai."

I know he is right. There is little that is difficult about multiple trees, rock plantings, even seasonal assemblies that are later broken up. The techniques you learn for single trees carry you most of the way, and the few special tricks are surprisingly easy to master.

Multiple plantings go by a variety of names—clusters, groves, groups, forests—each suggesting the number of trees used. A cluster contains the least, usually only three to five, and a forest the most, perhaps a dozen or more.

MULTIPLE PLANTINGS

Aside from their immediate beauty and the fact that well-planted multiples become more lovely with age, most of them offer a practical benefit. Group plantings are an ideal way to make good use of immature seedlings and also of less-than-perfect trees. These are busy compositions and small imperfections go unnoticed or can be trimmed away.

Multiples become more lovely with age as shown by this young Ezo spruce planting. Dr. and Mrs. Francis E. Howard.

The masterful simplicity of this grove of Japanese black pine makes it an outstanding example. Henry Fukuchi.

Some growers categorize multiple plantings as natural, formal, or artificial. A *natural* is a re-creation of a forest. Trees are angled in various ways. Roots may be intertwined. *Formal* plantings are arranged along traditional, organized lines. The *artificials* include miniature buildings and figures, and resemble bonkei or saikei. These are discussed in Chapter 14.

With multiples the first step is to decide upon content and perspective. Will you assemble a glade, a grove, a forest? Should the scene be set on a mountain, a slope, or in a valley; the view distant or close? There are so many exciting possibilities. About the only thing you can't do is combine approaches. A multiple planting must have a clear-cut point of view.

SELECTING
TREES AND CONTAINERS

The trees you use influence scale and perspective. Some are suitable for close or for distant scenes, others are right for only one perspective. Small-leaved plants are usually best for multiple plantings, although large-leaved types may not be out of place in close-ups. Some growers choose trees whose new leaves are lighter than the old, because the color contrast is interesting. Others prefer trees from the same clone— that is, descendants from one seedling—because their uniform growth suggests a uniform environment. Since most grove plantings must be shallow-rooted, trees that can stand heavy root-pruning are the most adaptable.

Among evergreens good choices include: smaller-leaved native junipers, imported needle juniper, Japanese cedar, Hinoki cypress, Ezo spruce, and cryptomeria.

Deciduous possibilities include: small-leaved beeches, as the European *Fagus sylvatica,* birch, hornbeam, larch, zelkova, and Japanese and trident maples. (Dwarf maples are inappropriate, the growth too shrubby and dense.) Flowering trees are rarely suitable since leaves and blooms are out of scale. The one exception that comes to mind is *ume* or *mume,* the Japanese flowering apricot.

If you make your grove with one species, it will be easier to style and maintain. Combinations, especially of conifers and deciduous trees, don't look right. You just might be able to put some other evergreens with some deciduous species, but the difference in growing rates is likely to prove troublesome. Constant trimming would probably be required to keep one species from blotting out another.

Although no container is exclusively associated with multiple plantings, those most commonly used are shallow (to make the trees seem tall), long, and oval or rectangular. The best are simple with little or no ornamentation. However, clusters can look attractive in ornate "petal" or hexagonal pots. Dished or hollowed rocks make good containers, their character in keeping with the plantings.

To avoid symmetry, work with odd numbers—in the total number of trees and also in the number of subordinate groups. Imbalance is more interesting than balance, and a variety of sizes and shapes less likely to appear planned and static. Let one tree dominate by size and placement; if you use groups within the grove, let each include a dominant specimen. Variations can produce a pleasing visual rhythm; on a literal level, they give the impression of parent trees surrounded by children.

Depend upon the concept of thirds. Set strong elements off-center, at a point equal to one-third the length of the container. If you can devise changes in soil levels, you will add interest. Evolve triangles on horizontal and vertical planes. Let trunks appear vertically in repeated triangles; when possible, let smaller groups add up to a larger one. As you look at the planting horizontally, the foliage should create still other triangular impressions.

Good plantings are tightly composed. In fact, the best are likely to fall apart when even one tree dies. It is a good idea to try different placements until you find the most effective. Emphasize the "best" side of each tree, pruning or minimizing its less exciting branches. Keep in mind that spaces are as important—as visually active—as the filled areas. *Well-designed plantings always appear to draw space from beyond the container into the composition.*

Once you have settled upon a plan, number the trees, or relate them in some way to a keyed drawing. Then remove them and prepare the container as for standard potting. Since most multiple plantings require some support, I thread nylon ties (but wire can be used) through the drains before I start potting. If you prefer to depend upon outside support, wiring can be done last. The same techniques apply to multiple plantings as to single trees.

Raft Bonsai

Groves are not necessarily composed of many trees. One tree planted on its side can develop into a grove, called root-connected or raft bonsai in this country, and *netsuranari* or *ikada* in Japan. The common root assures uniform growth, and with deciduous trees, there is a period of dramatic fall color. Here are the procedures:

Deciduous or evergreen rafts Select a tree with several good basal branches *on one side*. These side branches will become the forest; remove all other branches. Take the tree from its pot, lay it on its side, and prune off any roots that grow upward. Then place the tree on its side in the pot, and cover the trunk to at least half the diameter. Tie the trunk in place until new roots develop to hold it. As branches grow, pinch each to one bud to encourage thick growth. In time, all branches will thicken to become the trunks of your raft.

175

A handful of young Japanese cedars and thirty minutes gave Jack A. Dutro this exciting grove.

176

5. *An aged Chinese elm is shown in a landscape setting with tiny bronze figures from the collection of John Naka. Ben Oki. Richard Gross photo.*

6. *In this country old native bonsai are rare for we have been collecting and training for a comparatively short time. This stately pink azalea is two centuries old, and was imported from Japan. Ken Sugimoto.*

This planting of pistachio trees will be improved after a planned thinning process.
Remo Zaro.

Conifer rafts With the tree already in a container, remove all branches from one side; select some on the other side for the forest. Wire them to the styling you wish. Then turn tree and container on the side—wired branches upright—and grow in that position for one year. In spring, remove the tree from the container, prune the roots, and place it on its side in a pot of prepared soil. Cover the roots and bury the trunk to half the diameter. Tie in place until new roots form.

Rock Planting

Rock plantings are often looked upon as a tour de force, a surprising bit of legerdemain. They are considered the most fantastic of all bonsai, yet they are one of the easiest. Major types are categorized as *rock-grown* and *grown-over-rock*, and these are reasonably accurate descriptive terms.

Rock-grown bonsai are planted *on* or *in a rock*, the rock often serving as container.

Grown-over-rock bonsai are designed two ways—with roots astride the rock like a saddle—"stone clasping" as the Japanese poetically call it—or with some roots attached to the rock, some reaching into the soil below. Position is usually considered a matter for subclassification.

As with grove plantings, you have a choice of perspectives for either rock planting. In the more traditional close view, emphasis is on the tree. In the distant view, the rock dominates. Tree and rock should not be of equal size, since equality produces a static effect. As with groves, combining plants lets you use materials that might not be good enough to stand alone.

Rocks or stones come from many places. Some are even imported from Japan. If you live in a city, you can buy rocks from a nursery or rock-garden specialist. I collect mine in the wild and thoroughly enjoy the search. I avoid river rock because it is smooth, and ocean rock because of its salt content.

Rough-textured rocks look best. Weathered, broken forms are often effective, and the surface will usually hold soil. Some growers dislike volcanic rock because roots may break it, but I've used it without trouble. Volcanic rock, being porous, does require more water, but its softness makes it easy to shape.

Select stones according to the roles they are to play. For a distant scene a rock should be more dramatic, and more nearly perfect, than one used for a closer view where imperfections can be concealed by a tree, ground-cover, or auxiliary plants. The Japanese often choose rocks of definite texture and color because these can contribute to a scene. For instance, a rock with a white streak can be placed to suggest a waterfall. In any case, every rock should have a flat, stable base. If it doesn't, try to have it leveled for you.

Multiples are especially appropriate on rocks. This is a "forest" of Japanese maples. Peter Ioka.

This Reeves tea-tree, *Leptospermum laevigatum*, has been planted on its side to produce a beautiful grove. Barrie Coate.

180

For rock plantings, choose species natural to your scene; cypress for a seacoast, spruce for mountains. Young trees are often a good choice to use for distant views. Older trees can be developed for grown-over-rock styles. In either case the best trees are those with dense limbs, for green abundance makes the strongest impression. Rough, over-sized leaves are never suitable.

In-rock bonsai are the easiest to plant since roots are placed in holes drilled through the rock. Drainage is no problem, and the rock functions as a container. If your rock is soft, you may be able to make holes yourself, but with hard stone it pays, in terms of time and frustration, to have a professional do the work. To plant, first cover the bottom of each rock cavity with quarter-inch wire screen, then partially fill with gravel, add potting soil, and insert the tree.

On-rock bonsai are not so easily planted since a tree must be held to the stone until it develops a foothold of roots; this usually takes six to twelve months. Techniques vary with the angles and contours of the rock. On gentle dished slopes, gravity and a clay soil do it, but on steeper inclines special "hold-downs" are required.

Hold-downs have two parts: rings attached to the rock, and wires attached to the rings and laced over the roots. You can make rings from medium-gauge copper wire, and for holding, use covered aluminum or fine-gauge uncovered copper wire. Since the rings must be buried, they should not be more than a quarter of an inch wide.

Some growers depend upon lead inserts to secure rings to crevices and holes, but it is easier to spot the rings where you want them with an epoxy glue from a hardware store. A dab will hold for years.

New ground-cover needs hold-downs, too, and you can make them from light-gauge copper wire. Bend the wire into U-shaped staples and press these into the moss. If you like accents, add small ferns, dwarfed azaleas, even ivy. One grower adds violets. He dwarfs them by constant pinching.

Special soil mixtures—clay and adhesives, for example—are necessary since soil must cling to the tree and to the rock against the pull of gravity. In Japan a mix is often made of powdered moss, black clay loam, and lake-bottom silt. This combination is hardly available here, so we've made workable substitutes, the simplest a mix of sieved moss, clay subsoil, and loam. The formula need not be exact so long as the result is sticky, To strengthen adhesive qualities, increase clay content.

The amount of soil you need will depend on the size of the tree and the angle of the rock. Work in as much as you can to nourish new growth, for the soil you supply at the start is all a tree is ever likely to have. If the soil does not stick because of the sharpness of the angle,

(*Top*), A host of grasses can do double duty, alone, or as ground-cover. Dan Buckley. (*Bottom left*), This grapefruit, grown from seed, is a good indoor *mame* plant. (*Right*), Another good indoor bonsai is this small but striking Sago palm, *Cycas revoluta*. Connie and Horace Hinds.

Utah juniper, *Juniperus utahensis,* was collected four years ago near Twin Falls, Idaho, and has been rock-grown for two years. Dr. and Mrs. Francis Howard.

try holding it with a fold of cheesecloth fastened to the rock. The cloth will keep soil in place until the tree grows roots to hold it.

If there is danger of erosion, cover the root-ball with a handful of sphagnum moss. Tie it around the rock. The moss will protect the fresh soil when you water. Later when roots are growing, you can replace it with a ground-cover.

To plant the stone-clasping type of over-rock bonsai, first wash the root system of the selected tree then spread a mixture of sphagnum moss and soil over the rock. Carry the mix down the sides of the rock to the soil in the bottom of the container. Place the tree on the rock and work the roots down to, or toward, the lowest soil. Wire hold-downs may be needed. If so, cover them with soil, then with moss. Tie the tree to the rock (and tie the rock to the container) with nylon string. In time, roots will grow down to the soil in the bottom. Then you can carefully wash the mix from the rock to expose the upper roots and so increase the artistry of your bonsai.

EARLY CARE

Water newly-made grove and rock plantings with a fine mist as soon as they are completed. Place them in a sheltered, shady area for three to six weeks; then gradually increase exposure to sun until they receive a normal amount for the species. Rock-grown bonsai will require the most water; through the summer, they should receive one or two extra waterings each day.

Repot groves when roots become crowded—every other year in most cases—but don't repot rock plantings. Tree and rock should never be separated.

House Plants as Bonsai

The evergreens and trees usually selected for bonsai can be displayed indoors for only a short time, usually less than a week. But there are a number of plants, from ivy and geraniums to herbs and grasses that thrive indoors indefinitely, and these also have possibilities. Ivy is a popular choice. Its woody growth readily adapts to bonsai training, particularly to flowing, cascade styles. The familiar English ivy is not the best choice because of its large leaves, but many small-leaved varieties, such as 'Emerald Jewel', 'Heartleaf', and 'Pin Oak', are excellent. Grape ivy, (*Cissus rhombifolia*) is also good.

Indeed, any woody-stemmed subjects that make good house plants can be trained as bonsai. Geraniums offer extensive opportunities. We think first of the dwarfs and the miniatures. I saw a photograph of the small 'Black Vesuvius' trained as a bonsai by Mrs. Clara May of Long Beach, California. It was a prizewinner, and its charm was unmistakable. 'Imp' and 'Small Fortune' also make good *mame* bonsai and even in age hardly go to three inches. But, generally speaking, miniature and dwarf geraniums, especially those with variegated leaves, incline

184

to be more difficult to grow than the medium-sized or larger zonals. Among small ones that are still somewhat larger than the dwarfs are 'Emma Hossler', 'Mr. Everaarts', and 'Tu-Tone', and these are of easy culture. The fancy-leaved geraniums also make delightful bonsai, and you might like to try 'Alpha' ('Golden Harry Hieover'), 'Blazonery', 'Distinction' ('One-in-a-Ring'), 'Jubilee', and 'Mrs. Henry Cox'. Among the scented-leaved geraniums, you can select for different fragrances. If the foliage is small, the plants are all the more adaptable, as the lemon-scented 'Prince Rupert' and the ferny, rose-scented 'Filicifolium'. The mint-scenteds have too-large leaves for easy training.

Then there are the herbal plants, as the aromatic-leaved *Iboza riparia*, which develops a strong woody stem in less than six months from a rooted cutting. Other good herbs to try include the true myrtle (*Myrtus communis*), rosemary, salvia, and lavender-cotton (*Santolina chamaecyparissus*).

If you have a sunroom or other place where the temperature is unlikely to rise much above 65 degrees, and there is a drop of some ten degrees at night, many of the handsome flowering shrubs are worth while, as the acacias, camellias, fuchsias, and lantanas. And very attractive bonsai have also been developed from the dwarf *Gardenia radicans*, the mistletoe fig (*Ficus diversifolia*), *Podocarpus chinensis*, the silk-tree (*Albizzia julibrissin*), various crassulas, and the sweet olive (*Osmanthus fragrans*). The climbing *Oxera pulchella* makes an unusual bonsai.

There are a host of other possibilities, grapefruit, for instance. Large bonsai appear in shows, and I'm growing a seedling as a *mame* now. Among grasses, horsetail-reed makes a good bonsai and bamboo can look marvelous. You might like to try Chinese goddess bamboo (*Bambusa multiplex*), fernleaf or stripe-stem (*B.m. diversiflora*), or the dwarf bamboo (*Sasa pygmaea*). Plant these as narrow root divisions and control size by peeling some of the developing sheaths. Indoors, grow bamboo at a sunny window. When tight clusters develop, usually in the second year, you may have to separate them.

In general, the trees or shrubs that thrive indoors as well as out are fine for bonsai, but most of the familiar house plants rarely make proper bonsai, rather they can be trained to bonsai-like forms.

(*Above*), An Hinoki cypress rock planting, one view. (*Below*),
Opposite view of the same Hinoki planting.

186

In a conventional container, a grown-over-rock bonsai features roots which grow down into the soil. Henry Fukuchi.

Rock-grown trees, among the most beautiful of all bonsai, are never separated nor repotted. Max Cann.

A rock, with a hole drilled for drainage, becomes a container for this Japanese maple.
Mrs. Emil Steinegger.

(*Above left*), "Hold-downs," made of medium-gauge copper wire, can be bent by hand or on this simple-wire bending tool. (*Right*), Epoxy glue secures the hold-down and allows you to place the tree anywhere you like. (*Below left*), The wire, which will hold roots in place, is fastened to the hold-down. (*Right*), An application of basic muck permits roots to grow in difficult areas; it sticks to the plant and acts as an adhesive to the rock.

13. Notebook for Enthusiasts

Here is a collection of photographs of some fine American bonsai with comments to remind you that the art of bonsai is highly personal and that success depends as much on your imagination as on your techniques.

Learn to see from various points of view. There is no completely right nor completely wrong way to style a tree. Two growers may see the same species quite differently, and both make successful bonsai modeled upon it. Two olive trees and three cotoneasters prove the point. The natural form of each tree dictated the design.

Olives In photo 1 the trunk of a twenty-year-old olive tree collected by I. R. Bilskey, conveys the sense of age, yet the trunk would appear abnormally thick and out of scale had he not left thicker-than-normal branches for balance. John A. Dutro in Photo 2 takes an opposite approach as he places a delicately-branched tree atop a hillside of moss.

Cotoneasters The three have one quality essential to all good bonsai —stylings that seem natural. In Photo 3 Barrie Coate has given his necklace cotoneaster linear styling that emphasizes delicacy. Contrast it with his sturdier, treelike treatment of the five-inch *mame* thyme-rockspray cotoneaster in Photo 4, or in Photo 5 with the positive, upright handling of a seven-year-old shrub by A. W. Blackhall.

Avoid complex designs; most of them are weak and confusing. By consistent pruning John A. Dutro made this beech in Photo 6 into an effective bonsai whose simple form has strength even in bare branch, a revealing test. Photo 7 shows how Bob and Peggy Krohn pruned away branches to reduce a Sawara cypress to its strongest form. The design consists of three branches clearly seen beneath the umbrella of foliage. At the base, soil crowns from the container to focus attention on the trunk.

Photo 1

7. *A twenty-five-year-old azalea flourishes with controlled sunlight in the protection of a lath house. Y. Sato.*

8. Bonkei, tray landscapes, are made of various artificial materials, the views imaginative or actual. The mountain site (above) is fanciful; the seascape (below) copies a picture in a book of famous Japanese scenes. For keto peat, used here for rocks and mountains, chopped asbestos (from plumber's suppliers) can be substituted. Colors and accents are brushed on with paint. Trees, boats, lighthouse, and bridge are tiny replicas, often made of ceramic. Both by Peter Ioka of Sacramento, California; as a child, he learned bonkei techniques in Japan.

Photo 2

Photo 3

Photo 4

Photo 5

Photo 6

Photo 7

195

CH. *13*

You can reduce the unproductive length of a tree by bending the trunk. In Photo 8, a mountain hemlock with a naturally-curved trunk was collected on a Kusamura Bonsai Club outing by Connie and Horace Hinds.

Photo 8

Photo 9

To keep the tree short, they wisely decided to continue the curve. In Photo 9, the Japanese black pine was trained by Henry Matsutani to its low form from the first potting. If erect, the distance from pot to first limbs would not be so artistic. In Photo 10, Dan Buckley trained a grafted Japanese five-needle pine to a modified *horai* style in a successful effort to reduce legginess. The tree was planted in a saikei container that repeated its twisted shape.

Photo 10

LOOK TO THE FRONT

Every tree has one side that is stronger than another, and this should be the front, from which a good bonsai design evolves. In Photo 11 you see the front of Yoshio Sato's flowering almond. The styling seems resolved, the lines, balanced. In Photo 12 you see the back. Styling is pleasing, but lines are not resolved. You feel as if you should see the tree from another angle.

Photo 11

Photo 12

Exposed roots are an indication of age. You can handle them in several ways. Photo 13 shows a very fine example of roots grown over rocks; Photo 14 an above-ground design strong enough to carry the styling. (Both Japanese black pine by Henry Fukuchi.) In Photos 15 and 16, Yoshio Sato lets roots of flowering almond create their own unusual form, and for contrast, uses ground-covers of moss and ferns. In Photo 17 John A. Dutro increases the effectiveness of a Japanese maple with a counterpoint of surface roots.

Photo 13

Photo 14

Photo 15

Photo 16

Photo 17

Sometimes select an unusual tree like Harry Lauder's walking stick in Photo 18, one of the few whose branches must be wired to make them grow *straight*. It makes a handsome bonsai for Connie and Horace Hinds. And what could look more natural than redwoods planted in a burl, as in Photo 19 by John A. Dutro?

Photo 18

Photo 19

In Photo 20, a six-inch *mame* Japanese maple is planted in a rare porcelain sake cup by Mrs. Leonard W. Renick. Mrs. Francis Howard potted a Japanese boxwood, Photo 21, in a fine cast-iron reproduction found in an antique shop. Mr. Howard made a wooden container for a lodgepole pine in raft style, Photo 22.

Photo 20

Photo 21

Photo 22

14. Saikei and Bonkei-
Tray Landscapes

Associated with bonsai are two other fascinating Japanese arts—saikei and bonkei, fairly new here, but with considerable appeal. Both are miniature *landscapes*, similar in their emphasis on realistic presentation. Saikei (sigh-kay) is more like bonsai, employing similar techniques and also live materials. Bonkei (bone-kay) is closer to sculpture, the materials, clay, paint, and reproductions of figures, cottages, boats and boathouses, bridges, and similar accents.

Saikei   Saikei is probably related to early religious plantings, but after World War II, Toshio Kawamoto, a Japanese bonsai-master, developed new concepts that made it a modern Japanese folk art. Many bonsai-growers find saikei an easy, natural companion for bonsai. Saikei is on a smaller scale, requires smaller trees, and offers a new use for *mame* seedlings. Since emphasis is on a number of trees and a realistic landscape, seedlings or imperfect trees can be used. As one writer remarked, "Saikei is right for pre-bonsai material."

FOR PRE-BONSAI MATERIAL   If you can create grove or rock plantings, you can turn to saikei with confidence. Even terminology—formal, informal, and cascade plantings, for example—is the same. The accompanying photographs show the similarity in techniques. One difference is the emphasis on rock. In saikei, it is the rocks that give the feeling of realism and scale.

ROCKS AND SOILS   You can collect rocks for saikei from many places—rivers, mountains, and deserts. Select stones for their texture and for their possibility of representing, say, mountains, islands, or a terraced hillside. Since a large part of each rock is to be buried, some defects can be hidden.

204

Scenes like this from the Oregon coast—photographed or remembered—offer inspiring designs for tray landscapes.

Figures, bridges, buildings, and other objects add realistic touches.

As you make your first landscape, you will discover the requirements are similar to those for *mame* bonsai. Pottings are the same. The basic mix, given in Chapter 3, is good (but add peat when yon need a more adhesive mix). Ground-covers for bonsai are suitable for saikei, as fine-textured mosses and grasses with short leaves.

Small ceramic or metal reproductions—figures of people and animals, houses, and wharves—can be introduced in the finished planting. You can buy these from various sources. I have ordered some by mail, found others in Japanese nurseries and Oriental shops. You can select painted or unpainted reproductions. The unpainted "mud figures" usually appear less intrusive in a small landscape. However, it is the scale of the pieces that is the important consideration.

CONTAINERS

Saikei containers, like those for bonsai, must have drainage. Some of the new free-form shapes are divided. One side has drainage, the other does not. These are made for land-and-water representations, and usually designed by Kawamoto. I am told by Dan Buckley, a West-Coast importer, that many of the popular saikei containers are now available in the United States.

When you cannot find conventional containers, look for substitutes. Flat bonsai pottery is a possibility, or with a jigsaw, you can make your own containers from waterprooof plywood. I prefer low wooden containers for many plantings; being shallow, they make the landscapes seem larger, and wood associates well with plants.

Potting and planting techniques are similar to those of bonsai. Try seedlings, container-grown if possible, so that roots will already be confined. Retain as much of the original root-ball as you can but spread out the roots to give each tree a solid footing.

Saikei are easy to make. Here are my own guidelines:

1 Select rocks with care. When you use one stone, be sure rock and tree are compatible. For good balance, usually place both on the center line of the container. Be sure the two move visually in the same direction.

2 Let height of stone relate to height of tree. Never lose sight of scale. Unless a rock represents a mountain, let the tree dominate.

3 When you use more than one stone, be sure the stones relate in size and material. It is difficult to combine stones of different kinds and textures. Harmony is essential.

4 Use ground-covers, but with restraint. If soil shows through in a few places, the landscape will appear more realistic.

5 Keep to basic bonsai techniques. The artistic objectives, such as branch positions and foliage shapes, are as effective in saikei as in bonsai.

Give saikei plantings the care you give bonsai. In summer, water them as you would *mame,* two or more times a day, and give protection from direct afternoon sun. In winter, water them daily and protect against freezing. I store mine in a coldframe.

Fertilize as you would *mame.* Pastes are good, especially if you allow one small ball for each planting. Liquids are effective. Dilute to a solution weaker than that recommended by the manufacturer. Apply on a twice-monthly to once-weekly schedule during spring and fall, on a twice-monthly to monthly schedule in summer. Don't fertilize during rainy periods or in winter.

Bonkei

Bonkei "the art of three dimensions" is increasing in popularity in Japan. It requires no difficult techniques.

MATERIALS

The first step is simple hand-molding. Beyond this first easy formation, the scene is assembled—rather than created—from various materials. Colored sand is sprinkled to represent water. Powdered soil is spread to represent earth. Ceramic and metal bridges, buildings, boats, and figures contribute to realism, and ready-made trees complete the scene. A well-made bonkei may appear to be a complicated work of art, but even a beginner can produce a good one in half an hour.

Make your bonkei on trays. They are called *suiban* in Japan and measure about one-by-three feet. But there are substitutes, and dimensions are not so important as proportions. Ingenious designers have used cookie sheets, baking pans, and serving trays covered with plastic; any not too flexible are good. Containers should not have drains since bonkei are moistened and must be kept wet. You can line containers with paper toweling to retain and equalize moisture.

Begin with a claylike material the Japanese call *keto* (kay-tow) peat, a vegetable substance sold in dried form. When it is moistened and kneaded to the consistency of thick dough, it looks and feels like a chocolate-brown clay. The peat is easy to use and can be reused.

While you can find *keto* peat in Japanese shops in some cities, it is not readily available. Instead you can use shredded newspaper as the Japansee often do. Moistened and mixed with clay, the paper resembles papier-mâché, but it is difficult to handle.

I prefer powdered asbestos, a material used by plumbers and heating engineers to protect pipes and ducts. Available and inexpensive, it becomes claylike when moistened. Actually, the difference between this asbestos and *keto* peat is in the color. Asbestos is gray, an unrealistic tone at best. The color can be masked by a sprinkling of earth, but when a specific color is important, I use household dye.

Final effect depends on accents of color, soil, and moss. Use tempera paints for highlights on mountains, islands, and foothills. Yellow, green, and brown are appropriate colors.

Collect soil and moss—rich brown earth and vibrant green moss. Dry them a week or more, work them through a fine-mesh screen, then store in bottles. Sprinkle them over your bonkei to indicate trails and grassy slopes.

Look for pebbles. Those white ones (not the colored type) packed for aquarium use are excellent. White sand is essential. I buy it from terrazzo tile-workers, the only ready source I have discovered. Colored sand, especially blue, is important. I make it from white sand tinted with water-soluble pigment. Dry pigments are available from most paint stores.

You can introduce living plants but artificial trees usually give getter scale. I buy mine from shops that handle reproductions, usually of wire and paper.

Few tools are required to make bonkei. The three I use most are spatulas. One from Japan was made just for bonkei. The other two are a double-ended spatula I discovered in a chemical-supply shop, and a putty knife. Buy two or more paintbrushes, one with at least a quarter-inch tip—excellent for leveling sand—a smaller one for painting highlights. Use pincers to position trees, shrubs, and small figures. A syringe will complete your kit. Use it to add water to the finished bonkei and also to remove excess.

You can copy scenes from drawings or photographs, or reproduce them from memory. The source doesn't matter, but at first, I found it easiest to work from an actual guide. Even a simple line drawing helped. One man's beautifully realistic copies are of such nationally famous attractions as Niagara Falls.

As with bonsai and saikei, bonkei can be displayed in your home, and for a longer period than the other two. Properly moistened about every other day, a bonkei should last a month or longer. Display bonkei as you might a bonsai, a painting, or a floral arrangement—at proper height, against an uncluttered background. You will discover that different scenes require different viewing elevations. Try your bonkei at various heights, then place it at the most interesting.

(*Above*), Drain holes are covered with wire-screen secured by copper staples. (*Below*), A layer of fine gravel provides drainage.

(*Above*), Rocks help to create the scene. (*Below*), They are partially covered by potting soil.

(*Left*), Douglas fir seedlings, roots trained to small containers, are inserted with extra soil and a moss ground-cover. (*Below*), The completed saikei features a ceramic lion, a bridge, and a boathouse.

(*Left*), Two saikei in wooden trays have good scale. Pete Sugawara. (*Below*), Cypress container and design by Peggy and Bob Krohn.

Wooden containers, easy to build, from molding strips and plywood, are well suited to tray landscapes like this saikei featuring Sawara cypress. Builder, Bob Krohn.

Two waterproof saikei trays made by the author from waterproof plywood with a jigsaw, the parts glued together. (*Above*), The oval sectioned top is finished with a border and fitted to a base. (*Below*), A tray with separated sections is planted with seedling pines to depict a landscape with land and water masses.

(*Below*), A ceramic tray, made by Kawamoto, a saikei-master, enhances a scene (*right*), featuring Japanese pines. Importer, Dan Buckley.

An accent of a ceramic cottage brings a touch of realism to this scene of Sawara cypress and rock in a fairly deep container. Harvey Olsen.

A threadneedle cypress in a deep pot and placed on a bamboo raft suggests a scene through the addition of a small house on stilts. Mr. and Mrs. Paul Jodian.

Keto peat is not always available.

222

Powdered asbestos, used by plumbers and heating engineers, makes a good substitute.

Mold asbestos with a spatula; shape mountains, and while material is wet (*right*), add color from light to dark tones with highlights on hills and peaks.

Color the sculptured island with tempera; sprinkle blue-tinted sand from a spoon; spread white sand (*right*), to simulate breakers on a beach.

(*Above*), Sift sand into areas the spoon cannot reach. (*Below*), Sprinkle pebbles to create a beach. (*Right*), Add powdered soil to suggest a roadway.

(*Below*), Artificial trees of various types, sizes, and shapes are better for bonkei than live trees. (*Right*), Place them realistically.

Place a house, fisherman, and a boat in the off-shore water. (*Right*), Add water in one corner so as not to disturb the sand—it should not be deep but just enough to moisten and give the appearance of reality.

The completed bonkei is full of interest; set before a painted background of clouds (*right*), it is even more attractive.

Plants for Bonsai

Taxonomy: *Hortus Second*, 1947, Bailey; *Coniferae and Ginkgoaceae*, revised, 1967 by S. C. Harrison; *A California Flora*, Munz and Keck, 1965. Species marked with a star (★) recommended especially for beginners.

COMMON NAME	GENUS AND VARIETIES	COMMENTS	SOURCES
ALMOND, FLOWERING	*Prunus* *amygdalus communis albo-plena*, double white *glandulosa*, also "flowering cherry" *sinensis*, double pink *triloba*, also "flowering plum"	Hardy, branched deciduous shrub, standard and dwarf forms; bloom white to pink, good fall foliage.	General nurseries.
ARBORVITAE	*Thuja* *occidentalis nana*, American *orientalis aurea*, Oriental	Hardy evergreen, yellow to yellow-green foliage, lacy in flat sprays, neat seldom dramatic; needs moisture and protection from sun to avoid scorching.	General nurseries; sometimes sold in cans.
ASH	*Sorbus* *alnifolia*, Korean mountain ash *aucuparia*, European	Hardy, deciduous upright, dense; small white flowers usually in May; bright green leaves yellow in fall; scarlet berries. European needs more cold to produce berries.	General nurseries.
★AZALEA	*Rhododendron* *lateritium*, Satsuki *obtusum*, Kurume *serpyllifolium*, wild-thyme	Hardy, evergreen and deciduous shrubs; Satsuki and Kurume very popular for bonsai; *serpyllifolium* has small leaves and flowers.	Kurume readily available; Satsuki may be limited to bonsai specialists.

COMMON NAME	GENUS AND VARIETIES	COMMENTS	SOURCES
BAMBOO	Bambusa multiplex, stripe-stem or fern-leaf Chinese Goddess Sasa pygmaea, dwarf	Some hardy below zero, decorative, vigorous, spreading grasses, not bonsai in strictest sense, but fun; 'Chinese Goddess' with open, delicate foliage; dwarf grows to 10 inches; hardy to 20 F.	Specialized nurseries; mail order.
*BARBERRY	Berberis buxifolia nana, dwarf thunbergii, Japanese verruculosa, warty	Hardy; small, bright green leaves, well scaled; buxifolia and verruculosa, evergreen; thunbergii, deciduous. Berries yellow to dark red.	General nurseries.
BEECH	Fagus sieboldii, Japanese sylvatica, European atropunicea purpurea, purple-leaf asplenifolia, fern-leaf pendula, weeping	Hardy, deciduous; dramatic buds, good bark, rich autumn coloring. Sylvatica has small leaves; sieboldii most popular. Considerable color variation in purple-leaf strains.	Purpurea and sieboldii available, others more limited.
BIRCH	Betula lenta, sweet birch or cherry lutea, yellow papyrifera, canoe or paper pendula, European, drooping populifolia, gray	Generally hardy to −25 F, deciduous. Most good as singles and groves. Lenta, yellow leaves, reddish-brown bark; lutea, light green leaves, yellow bark; papyrifera, white bark, not often grown as bonsai but exfoliating bark is interesting.	General nurseries.
BOXWOOD	Buxus Harlandii, Korean microphylla microphylla japonica, Japanese sempervirens, common or English	Evergreen, hardy in sun and light shade; slow growing, small bright green leaves. Japanese excellent for mame, Korean and English better for larger bonsai.	General nurseries; plants in flats for as little as 10 cents.
CAMELLIA	Camellia japonica sasanqua	Evergreen, hardy to 10 F; may need winter protection. Sasanqua better, a shade plant, white, pink to red flowers; japonica larger blooms, stiffer growth.	General nurseries.

237

COMMON NAME	GENUS AND VARIETIES	COMMENTS	SOURCES
CEANOTHUS, WILD LILAC	*Ceanothus arboreus*, felt-leaf *griseus horizontalis*, Carmel-creeper *purpureus*, holly-leaf	Hardy, some lose a few leaves in fall, blue flowers, important American native. Carmel-creeper has smallest leaves.	General or native nurseries.
CEDAR	*Cedrus atlantica*, Atlas *deodara*, deodar	Elegant conifer, hardy to zero. Atlas, with twisted branches and bluish tufts; deodar with softer lines, trains easily yet tends to return to original form when wires are removed.	Deodar generally available; Atlas may be limited to bonsai specialists.
CHERRY, FLOWERING	*Prunus campanulata*, Formosa or Taiwan *japonica*, Chinese bush or flowering almond *serrulata*, Oriental *subhirtella*, Higan or rosebud *pendula*, weeping from	Hardy to zero except more tender japonica, deciduous, symbolic of Japan. Many fine varieties, blooms white through rose.	General nurseries, most species; a few difficult to find.
*COTONEASTER	*Cotoneaster conspicua decora*, necklace *divaricata*, spreading *horizontalis*, rock *microphylla thymifolia*, thyme rockspray	Hardy evergreen with tiny white or pink flowers, small bright red fruit. Horizontalis and thymifolia easiest; divaricata more upright with red fall foliage.	General nurseries; seedlings and cuttings.

238

COMMON NAME	GENUS AND VARIETIES	COMMENTS	SOURCES
CRABAPPLE, FLOWERING	*Malus* baccata, Siberian floribunda, Japanese or showy micromalus, dwarf or Kaido sargentii, Sargent's, dwarf sieboldii, Toringo transitoria toringoides, cutleaf	Deciduous, hardy to −8 F, important bonsai species. Pink flowers on many; white on Siberian, Sargent's and cut-leaf; yellow to red fruit. Insect control essential. Cut-leaf most delicate.	General nurseries for most; specialists for rare varieties.
CRAPE-MYRTLE	*Lagerstroemia indica*	Deciduous, full sun, winter protection; avoid high humidity, a cause of mildew. Small leaves, good scale, crepy white to pink bloom.	General nurseries.
CURRANT	*Ribes* alpinum, mountain odoratum, clove sanguineum, red	Hardy, deciduous, unusual, worth considering; small pink to red bloom in clusters, but yellow for *odoratum*.	Native nurseries, or can be collected.
CYPRESS, TRUE	*Cupressus macrocarpa*, Monterey	Hardy conifer. Hinoki and Sawara excellent. Monterey exciting potential. Bald interesting—should be grown more.	Some species, general nurseries; others from specialists and mail order.
FALSE	*Chamaecyparis lawsoniana nana obtusa*, Hinoki *pisifera*, Sawara		
BALD	*Taxodium distichum*		
FIR	*Abies* concolor, white or silver homolepis, Nikko silver koreana, Korean	Hardy conifer, evergreen, prefers partial shade, should be grown more.	White fir can be collected; others available from bonsai specialists and as seed.
GARDENIA	*Gardenia* jasminoides, cape-jasmine radicans, miniature	Tender, evergreen, fragrant flowers; does not like sudden temperature changes. Miniature, with small leaves and bloom, best scale for bonsai; can be grown as a house-plant bonsai.	General nurseries, mail order.
GINKGO	*Ginkgo biloba*	Deciduous, hardy to 15 F; bright yellow fall foliage. Male better choice; fruit of female is odorous.	General and specialty nurseries.

COMMON NAME	GENUS AND VARIETIES	COMMENTS	SOURCES
HAWTHORN	*Crataegus cuneata*, Nippon *oxyacantha paulii*, Paul's double scarlet *phaenopyrum*, Washington thorn	Hardy, deciduous, slow-growing, a welcome addition to any collection, Washington with small, white bloom. May not produce fall color or berries in mild climates.	General nurseries, most species. Nippon only from bonsai growers in some areas.
HEBE, VERONICA OR SPEEDWELL	*Hebe buxifolia*, boxleaf *cupressoides nana*	Evergreen, hardy; needs some sun; red fall foliage on some.	General nurseries.
HEMLOCK	*Tsuga canadensis*, Canadian or common *diversifolia*, Japanese *heterophylla*, western	Hardy conifers. Western is good choice; a native, with fine needles, airy appearance.	General nurseries.
HOLLY	*Ilex crenata*, Japanese *decidua*, possum-hawhaw *Pernyi*, Perny *serrata*, fine-tooth *vomitoria*, Yaupon	Hardy; Japanese, Perny, and Yaupon evergreen, others deciduous; separate sexes, both necessary for fruit. Perny and Yaupon very good choices.	General nurseries.
*HORNBEAM	*Carpinus caroliniana*, American *japonica*, Japanese *laxiflora*, loose-flower *Tschonoskii* or *yeodensis*, Yeddo	Deciduous, needs careful summer watering to avoid damage to roots and branches. American has largest leaves, laxiflora the smallest.	General nurseries.
IVY, ENGLISH	*Hedera helix*	Hardy, evergreen, but with training limits; small-leaved like Hahn's best. Good with rocks.	General nurseries.
BOSTON OR JAPANESE	*Parthenocissus tricuspidata*	Boston, hardy, deciduous, large lustrous green leaves.	

240

COMMON NAME	GENUS AND VARIETIES	COMMENTS	SOURCES
JASMINE, TRUE	*Jasminum floridum*, showy *nudiflorum*, winter *stephanense*	Most are tender, but winter jasmine hardy. Jasminum deciduous or semi-deciduous. Trachelospermum, evergreen. Both valued for fragrant white or pink bloom.	General nurseries.
CONFEDERATE	*Trachelospermum asiaticum*, yellow star *jasminoides*, star		
*JUNIPER	*Juniperus chinensis*, Chinese *procumbens nana sargentii*, Sargent's *conferta*, shore *sabina horizontalis*, creeping *scopulorum*, rocky mountain *torrulosa*, twisted	Hardy conifers, among easiest to grow and train.	General nurseries.
LIQUIDAMBAR OR SWEET-GUM	*Liquidambar styraciflua*	Hardy to zero; deciduous, moderate growth, interesting bark, red-to-yellow fall foliage.	General nurseries.
*MAPLE	*Acer buergerianum*, trident *campestre*, hedge *circinatum*, vine *ginnala*, amur *palmatum*, Japanese *rubrum*, red or swamp	Hardy, important bonsai species, easy to propagate. Trident and Japanese a "must" for collectors. Vine maple, a western native, also good with small leaves and fine fall color.	General nurseries, bonsai specialists; vine maple can be collected.
*NANDINA, HEAVENLY BAMBOO	*Nandina domestica*	Tender, evergreen, delicate beauty, good fall foliage. Choose stock in fall to insure best color; fast growing; may become leggy.	General nurseries; cuttings.

COMMON NAME	GENUS AND VARIETIES	COMMENTS	SOURCES
OAK	*Quercus* agrifolia, Coast live dentata, Daimio glandulifera (serrata), Japanese marilandica, black-jack palustris, pin suber, cork	Some deciduous, all hardy. Bright fall color, beautiful winter branch forms. American species generally best.	General and native nurseries.
*OLIVE	*Olea europaea*	Hardy to 10 F, many possibilities; small, grayish leaves; trunk twists with age.	General nurseries. Old orchards in the West may yield trees.
PIERIS	*Pieris* formosa, Chinese japonica variegata, lily-of-the-valley shrub nana, miniature	Evergreen, hardy except nana north of Virginia. Japonica common choice; Miniature is excellent. Protect buds from cold. Good as cascade.	General nurseries.
*PINE	*Pinus* aristata, bristlecone contorta, shore latifolia, lodgepole densiflora, Japanese red koraiensis, Korean mugo, Swiss mountain parviflora, Japanese white or five-needle pentaphylla, Japanese short-leaved thunbergii, Japanese black corticosa, brocade	Conifer, a favorite, more than 100 species. A few like brocade grafted to black pine for bonsai. Uncommon American species, like bristlecone, offer unusual possibilities. Black pine hardy, good for beginners; red pine most demanding. Mugo very popular.	General nurseries; grafts, seeds; native species can be collected.
PISTACHIO	*Pistacia chinensis*, Chinese	Hardy if not too much cold. Prized for fall color; lovely as single or in grove.	General nurseries.

COMMON NAME	GENUS AND VARIETIES	COMMENTS	SOURCES
PLUM, FLOWERING	Prunus cerasifera, Myrobalan plum or cherry atropurpurea, purple-leaf salicina, Japanese triloba, flowering or almond	Deciduous, prime selection in Japan but can be imported only as seed. If growing only one, consider vigorous cerasifera, small with exquisite white bloom. Purple-leaf foliage ranges from copper to near black. Triloba has double pink or white flowers.	General nurseries; bonsai specialists.
*POMEGRANATE	Punica granatum nana, dwarf	Deciduous; orange-red flowers, lovely trunk, delicate leaves; needs winter protection. Red fruit, yellow fall foliage. Dwarf bears early fruit.	General nurseries.
PRIVET	Ligustrum ionandrum, evergreen ovalifolium, California vulgare, common	Hardy; don't rule out because of hedge use. A lovely plant, related to olive.	General nurseries.
*PYRACANTHA, FIRETHORN	Pyracantha angustifolia coccinea crenato-serrata	Evergreen, easy to grow; white flowers, fall berries, red to orange. Pruning improves fruiting. Full sun.	General nurseries.
*QUINCE, FLOWERING	Chaenomeles japonica, Japanese dwarf lagenaria, Japanese sinensis, Chinese	Deciduous, single or double bloom, yellow fruit. Long flowering may weaken plants, pruning off blooms helps. Needs sun.	General nurseries.
REDBUD, JUDAS-TREE	Cercis canadensis, eastern chinensis, Chinese occidentalis, western	Hardy, deciduous, not often grown as bonsai but excellent. Rosemagenta bloom vivid. Eastern variety turns yellow or red in fall; flowers become pods.	General nurseries some areas; native nurseries others.
REDWOOD	Metasequoia glyptostroboides, dawn-redwood, water-fir, or water-larch Sequoia sempervirens, Coast	Dawn-redwood, tender deciduous; interesting species; Coast redwood, unusual native, not often grown but effective in shows.	General and native nurseries; also along California's Redwood Highway, U.S. 101.

COMMON NAME	GENUS AND VARIETIES	COMMENTS	SOURCES
RHODODENDRON	Rhododendron fastigiatum, Chinese flavidum, amberbloom impeditum, cloudland myrtifolium, myrtle racemosum, mayflower rupicola, cliffplum williamsianum	Hardy, evergreen; many exciting possibilities; impeditum and rupicola with half-inch leaves; racemosum and williamsianum 2-inch leaves.	General nurseries.
*ROSEMARY	Rosmarinus officinalis, common prostratus, dwarf	Evergreen. Officinalis the culinary herb. Small leaves in excellent scale; naturally contorted trunk and shredded bark good.	General nurseries.
SPRUCE	Picea abies, Norway glauca, white glehnii, Saghalin or Glehn's jezoensis, Yeddo orientalis pungens, Colorado	Conifer, hardy, popular. Saghalin and Yeddo traditional Japanese choices; Norway, Colorado and its varieties good U.S. counterparts.	General nurseries; bonsai specialists; native nurseries.
STRAWBERRY-TREE	Arbutus unedo	Evergreen; spectacular, 2- to 3-inch leaves, small white flowers, red to yellow fruit. Winter protection needed.	General Nurseries.
TAMARISK	Tamarix juniperina, juniper odessana, Odessa parviflora, small-flower pentandra, fine-stamen	Deciduous, lovely leaves; parviflora, pink flowers and hardy; juniperina least hardy. All need summer shade.	General and native nurseries.

244

COMMON NAME	GENUS AND VARIETIES	COMMENTS	SOURCES
VIBURNUM	*Viburnum opulus nanum*, European dwarf cranberry-bush *prunifolium*, blackhaw *tomentosum Mariesii*, double-file	Deciduous or evergreen. Lustrous green leaves usually turn red in fall; white bloom in May, berries later. Sulphur-base fungicides may blacken leaves.	General nurseries.
WEIGELA	*Weigela florida variegata* 'Bristol Ruby' 'Eva Rathke'	Deciduous, hardy to 15°. Not often used, but good. 'Eva Rathke' has smallest leaves.	General nurseries.
*WILLOW	*Salix babylonica*, weeping *purpurea nana*, dwarf purple osier	Vigorous, deciduous, requires much water; fast-growing for bonsai. *Note*: Australian tea-tree (*Leptospermum laevigatum*) is not related but has similar form and grows slower, interesting substitute.	General nurseries; can be collected.
WISTERIA	*Wisteria floribunda*, Japanese *macrostachya*, Kentucky *sinensis*, Chinese *venusta*, silky	Hardy, deciduous, woody vine well suited to bonsai. Chinese usual selection; silky similar with velvety leaves. White to lavender flowers. Old plants develop twisted trunks.	General and bonsai nurseries.
*YEW	*Taxus baccata*, English *brevifolia*, western *chinensis*, Chinese *cuspidata*, Japanese *nana*, dwarf *media*, hybrid	Conifer, evergreen, popular and hardy. Formal, dark green foliage. Sexes separate, female bears fruit, best for bonsai.	General nurseries; imported varieties from bonsai specialists.
*ZELKOVA, JAPANESE ELM	*Zelkova serrata*, saw-leaf	Hardy to –8 F; fine for any collection; formal, upright, elegant. Interesting bark, yellow-to-red fall foliage.	General nurseries; bonsai specialists.

Source of Information, Materials, and Plants

Information	Source	Material offered
	American Bonsai Society P.O. Box 95 Bedford, New York 10506	Information on clubs and source materials; quarterly, *Journal of the American Bonsai Society;* annual dues $5.00
	Bonsai Clubs International 2354 Lida Drive Mountain View, California 94040	Information on clubs and source materials; the publication *Bonsai;* annual dues $3.00
	Brooklyn Botanic Garden 1000 Washington Avenue Brooklyn, New York 11225	Handbooks on bonsai $1.00 each; active membership $10.00; corresponding membership $4.00
Tools	*Source*	*Material offered*
	Okatsune Scissor Mfg. Co., Ltd. 18 Takuma-cho Innoshima-shi Hiroshima, Japan	Tools
Plants and Seeds	*Source*	*Material offered*
	Alpenglow Gardens 13328 Trans-Canada Highway New Westminster, B.C., Canada	Alpine natives
	Bonsai-Bonkei Nursery Mrs. Laurose Page P.O. Box 186 Dolan Springs, Arizona	Collected trees; guided collecting tours
	Daiichi Seed Co., Ltd. Shibuya P.O. 34 Tokyo, Japan	Wide range of rare seeds; many rare trees
	Gardens of the Blue Ridge Ashford McDowell County, North Carolina 28603	Native trees and shrubs; native ferns

Source	Material offered	Plants and Seeds
Jamieson Valley Gardens Jamieson Road, Route 3 Spokane, Washington 99203	Western native trees and shrubs	
Kenwood Nursery P.O. Box 247 Kenwood, California 94542	Native trees and shrubs; general bonsai plants	
Lamb Nurseries E 101 Sharp Avenue Spokane, Washington 99202	Evergreens—*Mame* and *Ko* sizes primarily	
Leslie's Wild Flower Nursery 30 Summer Street Methuen, Massachusetts 01844	Native ferns; fern spores Catalogue 20¢	
Mayfair Nurseries R. D. 2 Nichols, New York 13812	Dwarf conifers, dwarf shrubs, and ground-covers	
Frank Newland Route 2, Box 2914 Woodinville, Washington	Western native trees and shrubs	
Orchid Gardens Route 1, Box 441 Grand Rapids, Minnesota 55744	Native trees, shrubs, and ferns	
Donald Stryker Langloise, Oregon	Western native trees and shrubs	
The Three Laurels Route 3, Box 15 Marshall, North Carolina 28753	Native shrubs and ferns	
Wayside Gardens Mentor, Ohio 44060	Trees and shrubs: native and domestic Catalogue $1.00	

Source	Material offered	Materials and Plants
Bamboo Man P.O. Box 331 Saddle River, New Jersey 07458	Bonsai plants Supplies	
Dan Buckley 5215 Sandburg Avenue Sacramento, California	Tokoname pottery Watering cans Imported fertilizers Plants Catalogue $2.00	
Iyama Nursery 2633 Bridgeway Sausalito, California 94965	Plants Containers	
Ken's Bonsai Garden 471 Pagemill Road Palo Alto, California 94306	Completed bonsai Plants in training Beginner's materials	
Pete Sugawara's Montebello Nursery 1325 Fremont Avenue Los Alto, California	Plants Bonsai Saikei	

Source	Material offered
Susu-en Bonsai Co. 326 West 31st Street P.O. Box 3015 Erie, Pennsylvania 16505	Plants Imported and domestic Containers Materials One-day workshops
University Nursery 1132 University Avenue Berkeley, California 94702	Completed bonsai Plants in training Beginner's materials Containers
Western Arboretum P.O. Box 486 La Canada, California 91011	Started bonsai Supplies Catalogue 10¢

Index

Illustration references in heavy type. Color plates 1 and 2 between pages 64 and 65; 3 and 4, 80-81; 5 and 6, 176-177; 7 and 8, 192-93.

252

About the Author   Robert Lee Behme has been a professional writer and photographer since he was graduated from the Art Center School in Los Angeles in 1948. His articles and pictures have appeared in *Better Homes & Gardens, Sunset, Coronet, True, Field and Stream, Sports Afield,* and many other magazines. He is Western editor for Davis Publications (*Mobile Life* and *Camping Journal*). He writes on many subjects—outdoor sports, camping, travel, native plants, and of course, bonsai. The author lives with his wife and two sons in the Sierra Nevadas, 150 miles north of San Francisco in the heart of the historic Mother Lode where naturally stunted trees abound for collecting.